LIFE RE-IMAGINED

From Frustrated to Fulfilled

Keitra M. Robinson, J.D.

Justinspire
LEGENDS MEDIA

ISBN: 978-0-692-19931-2 (paperback)

ISBN: 978-0-692-19933-6 (ebook)

First printing edition 2018

Published by Justinspire Legends Media

A division of Justinspire Legends LLC

info@justinspirelegends.com

www.KeitraRobinson.com

Dedication

This book is dedicated to my parents Judy and Jasper Musgrave who never quenched my heart to dream nor my desire to chase one. The two who were my first leaders in faith and have always taught me to consistently look to the hills from which cometh my help. Thank you for your enduring love and example.

- Shorty

Acknowledgements

I am richly blessed to have a family that is a constant source of inspiration and encouragement. I'd first like to thank my husband, David, who has surrounded me with his support and love and who has made room for me to follow calling and seasons of shift on the path to purpose, vision, and a re-imagined life. Justin, Legend, and Sean, daily you inspire me to live a life and experience that exemplifies the possibilities of God when we cooperate with our faith and put that faith into action. You guys are the first to celebrate my triumphs, and you all have such sweet ways of showing interest in and being an encouragement with the things you see me set my hands to do.

I am grateful each day for a family that gives as richly as you all do.

Table of Contents

INTRODUCTION

Laughter is timeless, imagination has no age and dreams are forever.

-WALT DISNEY

There we were, newly relocated to Florida, no real contacts, no family ties…only a nudge we believed to be divinely inspired and a bold faith to trust the adventure. Bags packed, passports in hand and big, I mean super big smiles on our faces as we walked onto the deck of the Disney cruise ship…but, not as passengers! Instead, we were embarking upon the cruise as part of the principal cast hired for an actual Disney Cruise Lines commercial! Yes, how cool is that? A Disney commercial involving our *entire* family who, by the way, could not boast the type of industry experience as a family act at the time which might explain such a tremendous out-of-the-gate opportunity. This was all God goodness. It too was a first experience for each of us with cruising, so we undoubtedly had layers of reasons to be brimming over with a near tangible excitement from it all. Not a moment escaped me as I watched all three of our boys' faces locked into a place of sheer joy and pride as we entered the ship with the production crew.

1

Each of their eyes spoke volumes as they began to absorb the enormity of this unique experience they would share. I too was in total amazement at the complete wonder of God but in so many more ways. You see, not only were we in physical transition through our recent move to Florida; but man, we were in and moving out of a significant spiritual season of transition that relentlessly lingered…so at least it seemed to me! But transition, as uncomfortable and at times down right hard as it may be, is God's strategic way to "re-position" us. As we will talk more about along the way, transition is all about us cooperating with God's loving process of putting order and alignment to who and where we are

You have to *transition* to get *re-positioned* to carry the significance and weight of your purpose in each season of evolution and growth in your journey.

so that we are positioned for and can be trusted with greater levels of purpose. You have to *transition* to get *re-positioned* to carry the significance and weight of your purpose in each season of evolution and growth in your journey. So hold on dear sister if the ride seems a bit enduring at the moment, there is a gift in the process, and there is another side. Just trust me on that. But here we were delighting in God's generous and heavenly wink. This indeed had God's redeeming signature and grace written all over it. No contacts, new city, hey, we barely knew our way around our part of town at this point. As a mother, I also wanted nothing more than for the boys to quickly find their sense of stability and belonging in this shift and now they would actually have the unexpected and fun privilege of enjoying the experience together of filming a commercial with one of their favorite household brands known to kids and families around the globe for being a catalyst for family joy and happiness. Even more, a brand that had earned synonymous ties with being the "greatest place on earth" where "dreams really do come true"! Need I say their cool factor with new friends and community was now suddenly through the roof.

Now about that *dreams really do come true* part… this was indeed a dream deferred for me, but to a time and place that was far more significant by sharing the stage with my family and a crew I would have never imagined as a young girl full of big dreams and the hope of possibilities on the stage. It's just one product of my re-imagined life.

What was also a treat about this experience was being some of the first people to experience Disney's "re-imagined" cruise ship as it was being re-released. Essentially, the same cruise ship is re-designed and up-leveled in its brilliance, capacity, presentation, and services to adjust to increased expectation, growth, wear and tear and evolution of people, technology and the brand itself. We see this in marketing with fresh logos, customer experiences, re-branded offices, stores and the like. Actually, we see this a lot in the brilliance and example Christ set forth in biblical narratives where He was the same but yet strategically and effectively adjusted the delivery of his message and his approach based on his audience and the needs of the people. There is no doubt a Master-full connection to harnessing the wisdom in growing in our ability to embrace our own evolution, stay connected to the core vision, and re-imagine how our evolved selves will walk out our purposes and make our impact in our various spheres of influence. This book is about learning to do just that while first gaining insight on principles of purpose and vision that are foundational to our ultimate sense of fulfillment. Now speaking of fulfillment, it's an eleven-letter word that yet carries a lifetime of meaning. It's an ultimate longing. Longing for our presence on this earth to be so effectual and aligned that we end up gaining a sense of satisfaction that is complete and reverent.

> **Fulfillment empowers you with a strong sense of purpose, satisfaction, and service.**

Fulfillment is not about a perfect life, but a satisfying one or what I like to say is a "well done" life.[1] Fulfillment graces you with a sense of comfort that your motivations are pure and your steps are sure. Fulfillment empowers you with a strong sense of purpose, satisfaction, and service. That is the framework of fulfillment that we will work from in the pages ahead.

Now the use of the language "re-imagined" is very inspired. Ultimately this book, your personal journey and your success in it are largely about recognizing your evolution and shifting your journey and how you deliver your unique impact based on that evolution. But you

---

[1] Matthew 25:23 His Master replied, "Well done good and faithful servant."

can't get there without engaging your imagination and setting a vision. The revelation here is that the success of our journey is about developing the skill to re-imagine those visions at various stages as we evolve so that we can begin to increase our capacity for higher levels and dispensations of ability and focus towards our next levels of purpose. It's an adventure, it's shifting, and it can be wondrous even in the unexpected leaps and turns of the ride with an empowered perspective at heart. My hope is that this book also provides that all-important perspective for you.

The first part of the book is about vision and will equip you with insights on the significance, anatomy and life-changing impact of a well-nurtured vision. We will also take a journey together by way of my own miraculous journey to encourage and empower you on how to give birth to and maintain a vision for your life. I can't wait to jump in! But before we do, also know that once we move through the foundational skill set found in part 1, the second part of this book is committed to completing the picture and shift from frustrated to fulfilled by walking you through valuable mindset principles you'll need to harness your power to "re-imagine" your life. I'm rubbing my hands together with giddy excitement about this journey we will take together!

Finally, part 3 of the book is where you will find a self-coaching reflection guide and journal developed to help you begin to apply the principles you have gained throughout your reading and uncover or update vision in your life. This section is also about helping to train your way of thinking towards living out your journey as a woman of vision. Know that this part of the book is as valuable as any other. Applying what you have gained and journaling your thoughts allows you to write and talk with God as you reflect on your reading and the revelations you find specific to your life. Here you will have the opportunity to process your inspirations and meditatively consider coaching questions as you allow the Holy Spirit to help you gain personal clarity, insight, and motivation.

As we turn the page to begin our journey, read with expectation, read with reflection and read with a prayerful heart. Ask God to speak specifically to your experience as we grow through this journey together that we will find between the pages of this book. If I could give you one measure of advice to gain the most out of our travels, it would be to simply commit to yourself. Where you are encouraged in this book to pause and reflect...pause and reflect. Where you are encouraged to prayerfully consider...prayerfully consider. Where you are encouraged to be active in the pursuit of your re-imagined life or to do the work...do the work. I promise you the gains will far out way the intention you will invest in obtaining every transformative drop from this guide that you can.

> **Ask God to speak specifically to your experience as we grow through this journey together**

So with that, I pray you are thoroughly blessed, enlightened and transformed by the words God has left for you in these pages. It has been my earnest prayer that every single word of this book is inspired by the Father just for you. That He directs every woman to whom this book is intended to these very pages. And that His presence is felt and his voice is heard as we take this journey together. Know my friend that you are greater than every setback, stronger than every struggle and more gifted than you realize. Your greater days lie ahead so let's do the work to seize them!

PART 1

THE POWER OF VISION
~THE SKILLSET~

"Champions are made from something they have deep inside them- a desire, a dream, a vision."

-MUHUMMAD ALI

CHAPTER 1

The Cure

The only thing worse than being blind is having sight but no vision.

- HELEN KELLER

Vision and how the eye can somehow process light to actually produce images and sight is a dazzling and complex phenomenon. Ever tried one of those cool vision tests where you stare at an image for a certain amount of time and then cast your eyes away from it onto to a plain white background? Magically, the image reappears on the new background on which you are focused right before your eyes! It's crazy! The sophisticated structure of our eyes and complex way in which the eye and our neurological system process light to create sight is quite amazing. I'm no visual expert, so no high-level explanation here, but the basic reason that phenomenon is possible is because photoreceptors deep within our eye on the wall of the retina will continue to fire-off if they have been stimulated by the light that has produced the image for long enough. If in that deep place of the eye, an image has been processing for a sufficient amount of time, the eye continues to function as if you are still focused on the image even after you shift your focus and attention elsewhere.[2] That's a lot like our envisioned futures or the vision that is projected from our hearts and not our eyes. So too it is that when we focus on those visions, when we take them to heart and when we reach a level of deep intimacy with them, even when our eyes and our focus are driven away and distracted from them, vision can still have an enduring way of consistently showing up and nudging our hearts. Vision is sustaining, and it is powerful.

Vision is sustaining, and it is powerful.

Frustration and those feelings that we aren't quite aligned, the experience that life is directing us rather than us directing our lives, a persistent state of being in neutral rather than in drive and a sense that our happiness isn't quite complete…these are all indications of a lack of vision. Vision is the cure to the frustration that can be wrapped up in seasons like these. In fact, many of us are familiar with the wisdom of Proverbs 29:18 that "where there is no vision, the people perish." But the second part of the verse which often garners must less attention connects our actual countenance to the powerful gift of vision.

---

[2] https://www.illusionsindex.org/ir/negative-afterimages

The verse goes on to share that "he (or she) who keeps the law or [keeps what God reveals], *"happy" is he."* So the key is first to get a vision and have a revelation and clarity towards it. But secondly, we want to be ever aware that from that vision there is a powerful perspective we obtain when we can live and walk in the revelation of God's word for our lives expressed through that vision even to the point of balancing our resolve and sense of happiness. In fact, let's see this principle come to life and demonstrated through the life of King Jehoshaphat for a moment.

~

2 Chronicles 20: 1-4, 12, 14-23

1Now it came about after this that the sons of Moab and the sons of Ammon, together with some of the Meunites, came to make war against Jehoshaphat. 2Then some came and reported to Jehoshaphat, saying, "A great multitude is coming against you from beyond the sea, out of Aram and behold, they are in Hazazon-tamar (that is Engedi)."3Jehoshaphat was afraid and turned his attention to seek the LORD, and proclaimed a fast throughout all Judah. 4So Judah gathered together to seek help from the LORD; they even came from all the cities of Judah to seek the LORD.

5Then Jehoshaphat stood in the assembly of Judah and Jerusalem, in the house of the LORD before the new court,6and he said, "O LORD, the God of our fathers, are You not God in the heavens? And are You not ruler over all the kingdoms of the nations? Power and might are in Your hand so that no one can stand against You. 7"Did You not, O our God, drive out the inhabitants of this land before Your people Israel and give it to the descendants of Abraham Your friend forever? 8"They have lived in it, and have built You a sanctuary there for Your name, saying, 9'Should evil come upon us, the sword, or judgment, or pestilence, or famine, we will stand before this house and before You (for Your name is in this house) and cry to You in our distress, and You will hear and deliver us.' 10"Now behold, the sons of Ammon and Moab and Mount Seir, whom You did not let Israel invade when they came out of the land of Egypt (they turned aside from them and did not destroy them), 11see how they are rewarding us by coming to drive us out from Your possession which You have given us as an inheritance. 12"O our God, will You not judge them? For we are powerless before this great multitude who are coming against us; nor do we know what to do, but our eyes are on You."14Then in the midst of the assembly the Spirit of the LORD came upon Jahaziel the son of Zechariah, the son of Benaiah, the son of Jeiel, the son of Mattaniah, the Levite of the sons of Asaph; 15 and he said, "Listen, all Judah and the inhabitants of Jerusalem and King Jehoshaphat: thus says the LORD to you, 'Do not fear or be dismayed because of this great multitude, for the battle is not yours but God's. 16'Tomorrow go down against them. Behold, they will come up by the ascent of Ziz, and you will find them at the end of the valley in front of the wilderness of Jeruel. 17'You need not fight in this battle; station yourselves, stand and see the salvation of the LORD on your behalf, O

Judah and Jerusalem.' Do not fear or be dismayed; tomorrow go out to face them, for the LORD is with you."

18Jehoshaphat bowed his head with his face to the ground, and all Judah and the inhabitants of Jerusalem fell down before the LORD, worshiping the LORD. 19The Levites, from the sons of the Kohathites and of the sons of the Korahites, stood up to praise the LORD God of Israel, with a very loud voice.

20They rose early in the morning and went out to the wilderness of Tekoa; and when they went out, Jehoshaphat stood and said, "Listen to me, O Judah and inhabitants of Jerusalem, put your trust in the LORD your God and you will be established. Put your trust in His prophets and succeed." 21When he had consulted with the people, he appointed those who sang to the LORD and those who praised Him in holy attire, as they went out before the army and said, "Give thanks to the LORD, for His lovingkindness is everlasting." 22When they began singing and praising, the LORD set ambushes against the sons of Ammon, Moab and Mount Seir, who had come against Judah; so they were routed. 23For the sons of Ammon and Moab rose up against the inhabitants of Mount Seir destroying them completely; and when they had finished with the inhabitants of Seir, they helped to destroy one another.

～

In King Jehoshaphat's testimony, we can see that he was utterly distressed. And for a good reason! His enemies, the Ammonites,

Moabites, and Meunites, were all stacked up against him and his people and defeat seemed unavoidable and sure. And what about that prayer? King Jehoshaphat wasn't playing…He was frustrated! Lord, do you even see me down here? Are you aware of my situation? Aren't you "THE" God of the universe with all power in your in hands? Uhm, this is not what I expected!…

Perhaps King Jehoshaphat and his circumstances in one way or another remind you of your own at points along your journey. Where your circumstances begged the question, "Lord where are you and how did I get here?" But what we learn is that the king's strategy to reposition himself was to seek God intently for vision through prayer. You can tell that King Jehoshaphat was a man of fervent prayer because he spoke in such real and honest terms to God that he gives an indication of a relationship that had grown in deep intimacy, familiarity and communion. It's a good pattern for the relationship through prayer that we too should develop as women of vision. And it is in that seeking God faithfully responded. He revealed a vision that was vivid, actionable and motivating. In fact, we can see that after God's response, the king's posture completely shifts! Such a great picture is painted here in scripture. The enemy was still coming, but Jehoshaphat could now move through his current circumstances with a sustaining strength and perspective now that he had the confidence of his destiny and the focus of his vision with him. The scriptures say that he now started confidently declaring their victorious end among the people and organizing the troops to praise in advance of the manifestation with their expected outcome in mind. This was a far cry from the man of distress, overwhelm, frustration and fear. What an amazing difference a vision made for King Jehoshaphat and can make for you too!

Now, you may be slowly raising your hand to say, well actually, I have a vision for my life, I know what I want out of life, I have an inspired vision, but I'm *still* just frustrated. And I submit that sometimes we have a vision, but we have vision problems. We may have a vision, but the vision is

Sometimes we have a vision, but we have vision problems

incomplete. For instance, you may primarily focus on and have a clear vision for your career, but have you developed or cared for the other 6 areas of vision for your life? (We'll get there to share those areas of vision in just a moment so hang tight.) You may have a vision, but the vision is out of time. Have you revisited it and has that picture for yourself evolved as you have evolved over time and experience? Or perhaps the vision is not yours! You are living or believing in a vision that someone else has for you, one that you feel responsible to live, or that the world has for you, but not one that God has designed for you.

So then, let's delve just a bit further into what vision is all about. Vision is tightly woven together with purpose. It is the picture of your envisioned future that gives life and elevated belief to purpose. Purpose is often framed and asked in terms of "the" reason or "the" why of one's existence. But the revelation that I wish to empower you with as you move forward in your purpose journey is that there is a better question to be asked, and that is, what are my purpos*es* for this <u>season</u>? Consider purpose severally not singularly, and seasonally not permanently. The bible says, to everything there is a season and a time for every purpose under heaven.[3] So then, we want to be available for various and advancing purposes throughout our lives that may shift and evolve, as will we, in various seasons and stages of our lives.

> **Consider purpose severally not singularly, and seasonally not permanently.**

So then, vision is that inspired picture of purpose that envisions "extraordinary" outcomes generated by God-sized hope. Whether it a personal, corporate or church vision, vision should motivate you and others towards exciting and stretched results that push you beyond what you can naturally and presently see. Like the picture God created for King Jehoshaphat of his remarkable and God-sized defeat over his enemies, vision puts the wind of our extraordinary God behind God-inspired purposes and pushes those purposes into next level outcomes.

> **Vision puts the wind of our extraordinary God behind God-inspired purposes and pushes those purposes into next level outcomes.**

---

[3] Ecclesiastes 3:1 To every thing there is a season, and a time to every purpose under the heaven.

A quick sidebar about vision versus direction... I would be remiss in not taking a moment to share this important note with you about distinguishing between the two as we become even more vision-focused women. As we are inspired along the way to extraordinary possibilities and as we have vision uncovered in our hearts, we should be mindful of the proper season and whether God is inspiring our hearts with a direction or a vision. Otherwise, we may see a thing, even clearly, and move prematurely and out of season. Been there! Instead, we want to be careful to ask God in those times of inspiration whether He is giving us a direction, something for us to immediately put our hands to do, or uncovering vision, a picture of a future end to which we are to align our actions and hope along the way. Either way, it is a faith walk, yes. But taking steps to discern the season assigned to the inspired hope that we see helps us operate with wisdom and strategy that can navigate us around potential bumps in the road.

Both direction and vision from God are deeply motivating, so a helpful queue sometimes is to consider what kind of motivations flow from your inspiration. Direction often motivates with a sense of urgency connected to it. This book, for instance, was a direction. I knew to write it and to write it without hesitation. I could see what it would be about, the people to whom it was intended, and I knew this was a story He already developed. My job was to obediently move in God's "right now" timing. Vision, on the other hand, may not carry the same sense of urgency, but it does often motivate with energy and excitement towards what your heart sees even when the dream may be a bit intimidating because of the breadth of it. And because vision is so inspiring, we can begin to immediately move out of time and without proper preparation because of those motivations and not recognize God instead is setting our hearts to align with that direction, strategize and prepare for a future goal. Our family's relocation to Florida was a vision. We were inspired to move several years in advance of our actual relocation. We could see it; we were energized by it although we didn't have all of the answers as to how or know what God was aligning. But David and I were both inspired towards the same. We visited, researched and prayed for confirmation and clarity. We aligned our footsteps with the vision. It was several years until we knew without a doubt to actually proceed to make a move, but when it was time, it was time. That was vision.

The beautiful news is that even when we jump the gun so to speak, there is still abundant grace for us in our well doing. In fact, there may be times you may be nudged to try the exact same thing you tried before and which failed. Don't be afraid and don't let that voice of past failure drown the voice of God directing you in your correct season. If you are surely inspired to move out in dreams again that still rests in your heart but which failed before, recognize the power of a vision in its proper time and season. Looking forward, you now have a strategy to help you rest at the moment when pictures of possibility are inspired from within and seek clarity that will help you move with greater wisdom and strategic insight.

Now with that in mind, let's continue along our understanding of how we may have several purposes in our lifetime and how as we evolve so too may our purposes throughout the different seasons of our journey. For example, I understand that one of my assignments in this season is to inspire (teach and express a message of encouragement translated from Spiritual insights) people, especially women and women leaders, towards revelations of their purposes and Kingdom authority. Now, that is a slightly different mission and picture, let's say, straight out of law school. But of course, my experiences, maturity, training, and revelations were quite differently positioned then as well. There are some purposes in my present season and the vision I have before me now that I simply may have been too immature in my growth to receive at that time and risk aborting the vision for lack of wisdom, confidence or strength.

Being mindful of the power of our purpose in its proper season also relieves the frustration that we are operating amiss. That experience of feeling there is more that we should know about where we are going than we do. But it is in those places where we are seeking answers to questions that aren't synced with the proper season that we can cause weariness in the

> **Being mindful of the power of our purpose in its proper season also relieves the frustration that we are operating amiss.**

silence and needless frustration. And frustration is what we are working to squelch. God is a protector of purpose, and He honors His own principle of timing even for the revealing of vision and purpose in our lives. As with King Jehosaphet, when we are diligent to seek a purpose for our season, God is faithful to provide revelation to inspire our big bold Ammonite, Moabite, and Meunite defeating kind of visions.

With these foundations at heart, let's begin to capture what it means to have and how we can make sure we engage a "complete" vision for our lives. Ladies, this can change everything!

CHAPTER 2

Vision Problems

*Our greatest fear in life should not be failure, but in
succeeding in things in life that don't even matter.*

– DL MOODY

Vision helps us discern destiny from distraction, process from pitfalls and purpose from pleasure. Our internal makeup is designed to yearn for the strategic power that vision offers as a sustaining and directing force in our lives. As we have seen through one of our guiding scriptures, *without a vision, we perish*. Now that's significant. It's a scriptural reference that is often and readily referenced but the depth of which we certainly owe a considerate pause. So let's rest here for just a moment.

> **Vision helps us discern destiny from distraction, process from pitfalls and purpose from pleasure.**

We *perish*. Perish means to lose life. In other words, when we lack vision, our soul lacks sufficiency, has a longing, and is unfulfilled.

Certain translations of the scripture reference that without a vision, the people *cast off restraint.* So where vision would inspire purposeful direction, a lack of vision can have you misaligned, over extended and frustrated for missing purpose in the chaos of busy activity.

So then, even when we experience measures of success in our lives, it is still very possible to yet experience the contradiction of lack in our countenance when vision is a lacking component in our tool chest. But on the other hand, when we diligently seek to obtain vision and are also careful to keep that vision before us like a law that directs our lives, we have the marvelous outcome of also benefitting from a contented and happy heart as our reward. How brilliant is that! I have certainly seen it, scripture says it, and we have every reason to believe it! So now, with fresh perspective take a moment to meditate on this scripture as you let it and the revelation within it rest in your heart...

Where there is no vision, the people perish: but he that keepeth the law, happy is he. Proverb 29:18 KJV

So then, vision is no doubt an uncompromising component to a life fulfilled. But no different than you buying the latest and greatest gadget with all of its complexities and amazing capabilities, it matters little to have instructions if the instructions are partial or incomplete. Where you have the ability to operate within 50 different unique functionalities that compliment the other, but your instructions only contain information for 10 or 20. What a shame to have all of that potential but no idea how to tap into it! That is no different from vision for your life. If the vision for your life is incomplete and not tapping into the several dynamic areas of your life that make up the whole, then you run the risk of not operating in the fullness of God's gifts and intentions towards you. It's one thing to have vision for an area of your life, but it's another to have a *complete* vision for the whole picture of your life. And so then we see where we may even find ourselves to be visionary people, but may unwittingly leave room to operate with a sense of insufficiency or with a nagging sense of longing because we are operating without vision and a focused internal inspiration in significant areas of our lives.

Now another subtle but significant thing about incomplete vision is that it can also leave us motivationally malnourished in the process and unable to respond to the unique adventure and challenges of our journeys with the determination and strength we would most desire. I remember a time I literally struggled with not having vision in one of my eyes for a temporarily time. It happened that my retina in my left eye completely tore and I had to have it urgently repaired in order to avoid losing my sight in that eye permanently. Certainly an unexpected twist, but gratefully I had a successful outcome. But because of how quickly things moved after the tear, it wasn't until afterwards that I fully realized that part of the process was that for several weeks after the surgery, I would be unable to see in the eye as part of the healing process. So you can say that my vision for that time was incomplete.

Now, I can't explain it to you all, but the strangest thing would happen during that time. Whenever I was in dimly lit spaces, like a restaurant for example where the evening "ambiance" was set, I just got inexplicably annoyed and agitated. "Can somebody turn the lights up in here please, geesh!" It was annoying like scrapping the chalkboard with your nails annoying. Yes, I know the hairs just automatically stood up on your arms thinking about that, huh? Well, the truth is, that experience is metaphorically a lot like how vision (our envisioned futures) works. When our vision is incomplete, and we run up against darker moments in our purpose journey, despite what we may expect from ourselves, we can often find ourselves frustrated, annoyed and with limited endurance during these times. But if our inspired visions are more complete for our lives, we can have the benefits of the motivation and hope that keeps our eyes on the vision in that area of our lives and less preoccupied with the challenges and darkness in the room.

"Immeasurably More Than You Can Imagine"

"Now to him who is able to do immeasurably more than all we ask or *imagine*, according to his power that is at work within us."[4]

---

[4] Ephesians 3:20 NIV

I love Ephesians 3:20 and the empowerment of this scripture when we consider vision, especially "complete" vision for our lives. The beauty here is that when we take a look at the power of vision through the lens of this scripture, we see that our omnipotent God is interested and able to immeasurably exceed our *imagined* futures, *but*

You think and imagine great; God performs greater!

it is according to the power *that is at work within us.* So first, let's consider here our thoughts and imagined futures. We see through Paul's inspired words that what it is that we think and imagine about ourselves are the root of God's "immeasurably more than" in our lives. You think and imagine great; God performs greater!

Now looking to the second part of the verse that speaks to the power that is at "work" within us. That word "work" here means "energized,"[5] or active within us. We energize that miraculous power resident within us as believers of Christ through revelation (uncovering, a bringing to light)[6] of the grace (undeserved favor)[7] of our Father towards us. We activate God's power within us by honoring his redemptive works as we learn to rest in and receive the gift of God's grace towards us. And for many of us, we may find that entering into that "rest" may not be quite as easy as it sounds. For others, we may

---

[5] http://www.biblehub.com/greek/1756.htm
[6] https://www.biblestudytools.com/dictionary/revelation/
[7] http://biblehub.com/str/greek/5486.htm

not be as conscious as we should of our challenges with receiving the gift of God's unmerited grace. So we must be diligent to constantly detox ourselves from the natural tendency of our flesh to merit or earn what grace is already positioned to do and has already worked out on our behalf. We can't earn what has already been freely given. So put the power of honoring God's finished works of "immeasurably more than" and grace to work in your life!

Therefore let us be diligent to enter that rest, so that no one will fall, through following the same example of disobedience. Hebrews 4:11

We also energize the power within us through our faith in our imagined futures (visions). Our faith and hope towards the manifestation of the vision before us is activating and stirs up the power of God within us. Like Shadrack, Meshach, and Abednego in the book of Daniel 3: 17-18, they confidently told king Nebuchadnezzar that their "God is able" to deliver them from the fiery furnace. "But even if he doesn't"… Now *that's* what power activating faith looks like. It's faith focused not on what God does but on what you believe He can do. And indeed they saw the manifestation of the deliverance in which they hoped.

But here is the deal. What if we don't have a vision upon which to activate and focus that hope? Power is then just waiting and available within us to be put to work towards a purpose we haven't yet assigned to it through the creative gift of our imagined and God inspired visions. We haven't formed the foundation through our thoughts and imagination for the wondrous collaborative work of God to unfold with the abundance and grace expressed in the "exceedingly abundantly above" measure. And I don't know about you, but I don't want to miss out on a thing God has for me!

So with that, let's empower our sense of endurance and fortitude strategically with complete vision. There are seven areas of what I like to call "360 vision" or vision that touches on a full circle picture of our lives. These areas include: (1) Faith, (2) Family/Relationship, (3) Personal, (4) Professional, (5) Financial, (6) Health, and (7) Service.

Now God in His infinite wisdom and grace may only inspire enough vision in each of these areas of your life that you have the capacity to receive at the time because as we mature through our journeys from glory to glory, so too His revelations to us. But, even so, God's order is that of completeness, wholeness, and abundance. And He is very interested in us aligning ourselves consistent with his nature by seeking him in a complete, well-rounded way with regards to vision.

God's order is that of completeness, wholeness, and abundance.

You can accomplish that when you keep these seven areas of vision in mind. Because vision is a spiritually inspired product of what is in the quiet of our hearts, you will also find your zeal, motivation, faith and contentment shift as you empower your thoughts with a holistic God-inspired vision.

To get you well on your way to being equipped with a complete 360-vision for your life and operating at higher levels of fruitfulness and fulfillment, I have developed for you a coaching resource that is designed to help empower your "complete vision" success in part 3 of the book. It is a self-guided coaching and reflection tool that will help you gain greater awareness and clarity on the visions resting in your heart and prompt your process of vision casting for each area. I can't wait for you to take advantage of it! In fact, feel free to take a moment and scan it now if you wish. But know that I was quite purposeful in placing this important resource after your reading so that you can first take in all of the insights and strategies that are part of our entire journey here and then with intention you can create the right environment and time in which to rest reflectively and meditatively as you invite God in with you on that experience.

CHAPTER 3

Going Deeper:
Giving Birth To Vision

"Cherish your visions and your dreams as they are the children of your soul, the blueprints of your ultimate achievements."

- NAPOLEON HILL

Now here is probably a good time for me to come clean. I should admit to you that this book and these principles, specifically, this matter of vision is not only a matter of revelation and inspiration from which I share, but vision is what quite literally saved my life! I know the power of vision first hand. I know that it can push you to extraordinary outcomes. I know it is a divine, power-packed, weapon of destruction to defeated living and low-level outcomes. God has

> I know that it can push you to extraordinary outcomes. I know it is a divine, power-packed, weapon of destruction to defeated living and low-level outcomes.

walked me through a journey that has given fresh insights on how to obtain and manifest vision that I am fully aware was not for me alone.

While I was pregnant with my second son, God orchestrated a journey that would generously give witness to not only His tremendous power and grace but reveal lessons of vision that would make all the difference in my life and I believe will make a significant difference in yours as well.

Both my son and I were given very little chance to live, and daily, the odds stacked up against us in rather sudden and dramatic fashion. Our journey was the stuff that prime medical lessons were made of, and as a result, local medical students began to make their rounds to our room to learn from the rare bundle of complex issues we were facing. Not exactly a way I envisioned being of service to the next generation but I'm always open to fresh ideas. Yes my friend, it was pretty bananas. But even then, there was a resolve, and a focus that I can acknowledge in hindsight was nothing but divine empowerment that allowed me to recognize even in that process that our journey was not as much about us, but what others would gain by it.

So over the next several pages, I want to share with you that journey and empower you with 3 key vision strategies that I learned during that time that helped me not only give birth to vision but also manifest the beautiful, amazing purpose(s) that were a part of the vision. So let's go deeper into the "how" of both obtaining vision and then manifesting the envisioned outcomes and purposes of that vision.

~ Giving Birth To Vision ~

I believe some moments, days, and events stick in our minds with pristine clarity because they are purpose moments. Moments that mark the time, or carry divine significance, or that are important in orchestrating our paths and giving wind to our direction even when we are unaware. Well, that is exactly what I think of that day I was driving down I-65 in Nashville, TN. The radio was off while I silently drove home from work and decompressed from the day. And all of a sudden, I got it. I called my friends to share the fun news. "His name is Legend! I just got it! It just came to me!...Legend!"

Well, I was around 4 months pregnant, and that name came to me out of nowhere. But, it was a name of which I was sure. "Legend Christopher Robinson." However, clearly not everyone else got the memo, and admittedly I did get a little shaken when I mentioned it to a few friends thinking they would be equally as excited about that name as me. But let's just say the name was met with a little bit of resistance. "That's a big name to live up to!" …"Uhm, I think you need to think and pray on that one again girl!"… "Kei, it's cute, but I don't know about that…" Ha! I have to admit, the wind was taken out of sails a bit. But I was going with my gut.

As it would be, just a few weeks later, everything went from 0 to 100 and fast! I was relaxing with the family at home, and the next hour I was being admitted to the hospital hemorrhaging at only 19 weeks of pregnancy. After some television-like scenarios, I was eventually placed in a room as we waited to hear further from the doctor. When she entered, she sat down beside me on the bed, placed her hand on my leg while my husband David (equally muddled) stood there beside me, and she began to share with great care her prognosis. "Well, you know there is no way your baby can live now, but that doesn't mean we can't believe for a miracle." A what? A miracle? Wait, what just happened? As dramatic as the preceding hours had been and as crazy as it may sound, it still had never occurred to me that we were "in trouble." One minute I was enjoying time at home with our 2-year-old, Justin, and my husband and the next moment the doctors are telling us that our pregnancy will likely not survive the night. Things were happening far quicker than we were able to process. But what I didn't know, was that moment would be good compared to the circumstances that would evolve. If things looked uphill then, they were impossible by the end.

Now, if you are pregnant or believing God for a child, let me pause here for a moment as I want to consider with sensitivity those sisters who are on their journey to motherhood. I have also been in too much spiritual warfare not to know the wisdom in doing so and protecting our atmosphere as together we take on important work towards walking out your next levels of purpose and success. So know that this testimony speaks to our position of victory and amplifies God's authority and power. I want to be very clear to speak that direction to your heart and mind so that the enemy has no room to disillusion you through fear from God's higher purposes in having your attention rest on the pages of this book. So for you, I want to begin with the end in mind and know that the end is that God fought and won our battle! Rest easy and receive what God has for you here.

So with that little business in order, my journey was much like King Jehoshaphat's and the people of Judah in that the Moabites, Ammonites, and Meunites that came to wage war against my tribe and our purposes were also multiple enemies. One of the giants stemmed from a rare complication called placenta percreta. Placenta previa is a more common and related condition in which the placenta of the womb is essentially misplaced in the uterus and covers the cervix where the baby would be delivered. But that condition can be graduated based on how deeply the placenta is incorrectly lodged into the uterine wall, and in the most rare of cases, less than 5%, the placenta completely innervates the uterine wall and begins to attach to internal organs close to the womb like the bladder.[8] Who would have imagined! Whelp, unfortunately, that's exactly were we landed- in that 5% "are you kidding me!" group. In the end, we had five surgical

---

[8] https://www.uwmedicine.org/health-library/pages/placenta-previa-placenta-accreta.aspx

specialists assigned to our one case to include a urologist to help plan and consult with regards to possible bladder loss or reconstruction and a surgical oncologist because of their advanced surgical skill. I was in good hands, seemingly a lot of hands, but really there were only two hands that counted most, and God had it under control even in the chaos at ground level.

Needless to say, I was hospitalized for the duration of the pregnancy. The concern was that with this degree of complication, most women do not survive even the ambulance ride to the hospital because of the severity of hemorrhage that can take place. So as tremendous a circumstance as we were facing, it was still God's grace that allowed us to discover what was happening before "the event." Most women unbeknownst to them can be hemorrhaging internally as was I, but unfortunately not understand the severity of their condition as it advances and not survive a more significant hemorrhage event. It's a rather painless condition with few clues. But in our case, we were warned of

The purposes inside of you are working to do the same and push through circumstances and seasons that would seek to bury them with defeat.

the battle that was on our heels so to speak. And it's encouraging to know that even through all of that, the purpose inside of me was growing, evolving, advancing in strength and fighting along. The purposes inside of you are working to do the same and push through circumstances and seasons that would seek to bury them with defeat so remain steadfast and encouraged dear sister.

One afternoon while I was lying in the hospital bed, I started giving Legend one of our daily team talks and encouraging him to be strong, that we would be just fine. This time, I felt that tiny little fella hiccup as I finished. Sweet little bumps in my belly in a steady tempo. His timing was perfect, and it was so amazing! It just seemed to magnify that He was so real, so alive and so baby. What a sweet gift to help me keep my hope big and believe beyond the mountains we were facing. I couldn't see him, but when he started acting like a little human, it certainly fueled my determination. Every day was a gift as we plodded along working to get out of the danger zone and to the place medical books consider "viable."

The purposes yet to be birthed inside of you have been giving you sweet moments of possibility as well. You too may not be able to see the manifestation of it, but those hiccups, those nudges, those reminders, still pop up to let you know that big purpose is still there.

Vision and the purpose that is resident within it are relentless.

That it is alive and still very connected to you despite the odds that are seemingly stacked up against you. Be it resources, opportunity, age, the lapse in time, or previous failures that are speaking to the impossibility of your vision, you must yet be willing and courageous enough to listen to the "hiccups", the reminders that the vision, those undeniable moments that remind you of what's still inside of you, are still waiting to be revealed. Vision and the purpose that is resident within it are relentless. You have to match your commitment to that strong heartbeat.

CHAPTER 4

3 Key Vision Strategies

~Strategy #1~
Listen To Your Heart

"Sight is a function of the eyes. But vision is a function of the heart."

- DR. MYLES MUNROE

The first key and matter of foundation with vision is that it is a matter of uncovering what is already in your heart. Purpose connected vision is inspired by God, it's inspired by what is in your heart, and it's inspired by your unique design in the way of skill, personality, talent, and spiritual gifts. You have a unique spiritual DNA that gives life to your unique visions. Your visions are assigned to you to give birth to so with that, we can get into trouble with matters of vision when we think in terms of devising a vision rather than "uncovering" a vision. Vision is not an outward projection, it is pulling up from within you what God has placed in and is incubating in the womb of your heart. As you will learn through the second key to vision in the pages ahead on how to get in position to uncover vision and gain inspiration for vision, the first key in getting there is to listen to your heart no matter

> **Vision is not an outward projection, it is pulling up from within you what God has placed in and is incubating in the womb of your heart.**

what your circumstances, well-meaning friends or even your own mind tells you about your "Legends". Like me, you may have powerful visions that you may second guess if you aren't careful to be heart focused along the way.

Speaking of Legends, God was doing his omnipotent work in aligning my heart and setting the atmosphere in advance for both affirming the vision and manifesting the vision when He spoke in advance of Legend's name. One evening one of the pediatric doctors assigned to Legend came into our room to consult with David and me and provide her thoughts on how to mourn his loss. She shared how important it would be for us to consider holding him in his death to help facilitate closure as we grieved. Should he live, we were warned of the potential likelihood of caring for him for the rest of our lives, brain bleeds, significant mental and physical disability, blindness and a host of difficult and potentially overwhelming possibilities. But, God had already spoken direction to my heart. He had legendary plans. Before we hit all of the atmospheric turbulence we would encounter, before circumstances unfolded in ways we would have never imagined or guessed, He already declared victory to my heart over the purpose. Legend means "one who inspires." Christopher means "bearing Christ." Hal-le-lu-jah! The outcome, no matter how crazy the circumstances might be, would have to bring inspiration and draw attention to Christ because God had already declared it to be so. And with that, despite the efforts of many to prepare us for what they believed to be the obvious end, I knew in my heart that a miracle had to be in the wings. God called him Legend before the purpose even manifested. This outcome would set precedent. It would be Legendary. It would have God's mark on it, and indeed it did.

Legend was born at only 25 weeks of pregnancy and just 1 pound 7 ounces. Born in November of one year (the week of Thanksgiving), he was due March of the next year. Despite all the possible and likely outcomes, despite all that he had to overcome by way of his prematurity while in the hospital, Legend is completely healthy, whole, wise and deeply aware of his story and His God. In fact, at the time of the writing of this book Legend is 9 years old and people know him as "Legend The Motivator"! He already spreads positivity, faith, and inspiration even through various forms of media

He will not speak louder to someone else about your vision than he will you, so listen to "your" heart.

from his heart to the hearts of many. The name Legend was indeed a big name to live up to as I was told, but God had already planned that he would! Your first vision strategy is to listen to your heart as it is imperative that you don't let life, people, circumstances, experiences, failures or anything talk you out of the visions God has spoken to your heart even when they are too big for you or others to understand. If you are seeking God, you will find Him.[9] And He will not speak louder to someone else about your vision than he will you, so listen to "your" heart.

How does vision speak to your heart?

In Psalm 37:4, the scripture says to "delight yourself in the Lord, and he will give you the desires of your heart." Many read that scripture to be that God is about the genie business. That if we commit our ways to God, he will give us everything we want. Rather, the word "give" in this

When you delight yourself in the Lord, He will put or set in your heart its desires.

scripture means to "put" or "set."[10] So then, when you delight yourself in the Lord, He will put or set in your heart its desires. And that's what we want. Purpose-filled, God inspired desires. If left to our own devices, we can desire much but desire amiss.

Undoubtedly we can also be heavily influenced by what it is that we see. We can begin to desire what we see of others, we can begin to

---

[9] inspired by Luke 11:9
[10] https://biblehub.com/lexicon/psalms/37-4.htm

desire based on the limited resources we see at the time, etc. But our

Purpose fuels the fulfillment tank.

goal is to be strategic with vision and purposeful in our journeys. Purpose fuels the fulfillment tank. So as we delight in God or rest in Him, seek Him diligently, and intentionally grow in our knowledge and intimacy with him, he will give us (or put) the right desires in our hearts.

Secondly, vision speaks to your heart through your "gut." Sometimes there is just a strong sense of knowing what not to do and what to do in our "gut." We just know and have a settled peace about a matter. Or we are troubled, and our gut is telling us to pull back. Your gut is powerful, and scripture tells us that when we free ourselves from worry and present our request to God that the *peace* of God, which passeth all understanding, will keep our *hearts* and minds in Christ Jesus.[11] That "gut" we speak of is our peace. Listen to your gut by paying attention to the peace of God. There are times when it comes to vision that you will have a deep sense of knowing and peace that you can't always explain, but those are places that you can't dismiss God's tender and internal way of speaking to you. I knew the name "Legend" was spoken over the purpose inside of me from heaven. I couldn't explain it, but I had a deep knowing and peace

---

[11] Philippians 4:6-7 KJV

about it. I listened, and that guided our course, gave direction for vision, and helped influence some critical decisions along the way.

So what does that mean for us as we live 360-vision empowered lives that are purposeful and fulfilling? That means we must be attentive to what our hearts are truly speaking. It means we must be courageous enough to honor those convictions and visions. And it means we must make quality time for God, seek His inspiration and expect that He will be faithful to inspire our hearts along the way.

CHAPTER 5

Vision Strategy #2
Shut the Door!

"If one is lucky, a solitary fantasy can transform one million realities."

-DR. MAYA ANGELOU

Simply put, everybody is not invited into the birthing room. Some intentional measure of solitude is powerful in the way of birthing clarity of vision and then maintaining that vision in our lives.

Undoubtedly, the crisis we were experiencing not only significantly affected us but significantly affected our family, friends, medical team, co-workers, and most anyone connected to us. I had been in the hospital long enough that the nurses had become friends, cared a great deal for our family and went out of their way to extend their hearts (and sometimes even their good cookin') to us. But what I soon began to realize was that most everyone began to operate and take on fear primarily attached to their love and care for us, but fear all the same. In fact, one of our doctors visited to update us on another significant development. We had many. From a transfusion that in simple terms also caused rare complications where my body began to reject the baby, to signs of infection that threatened termination of the pregnancy for fear of me developing sepsis or infection throughout my blood system. New news was a daily occurrence. So when the doctor visited with the latest update, it didn't take me by surprise. The warfare was intense. However, this visit did turn out to be different and a significant one for me as it shifted the course of my entire posture from that point on. As she began to share with me the latest developments, I noticed her voice began to crack a bit, tears began to form in her eyes, and then she actually started to cry through her words. "It always seems to happen to the kindest of people," she said. Now ordinarily there might be a nice compliment among those words, but in the midst of birthing a vision, those words were actually destructive and abortive. You see, I realized, she had already counted me out. I was a sure goner in her mind.

There are times in your journey when you are seeking clarity on the vision or when you have that clarity and are focused towards manifestation of the vision that you must be ready and willing to simply shut the door. Everyone is not equipped to match your faith and revelation of God's vision to you. So then, you must be ever vigilant and committed to create and maintain an environment where vision can be born and when it is born where it can be maintained and nourished. People, even well-meaning and deeply caring people, can snuff life out of vision through their fears and lack of faith. Jealousy falls in there too as it is just fear dressed in different clothing-fear of not measuring up, fear that plans will fail, fear of being overlooked.

So in order to make room for God to help you uncover vision and to help guard your heart during the birthing process, you must be willing to shut the door. Shut the door to negativity. Shut the door to fear. Shut the door to faithlessness. Shut the door to jealousy. Shut the door to distraction. Shut the door to naysayers. Shut the door! Now, this doesn't mean cut off and destroy meaningful relationships because good relationships are important. But this does mean own the courage

Own the courage to request room to seek, room to nurture and room to be supported in your birthing room

to request room to seek, room to nurture and room to be supported in your birthing room for the time that you may need. Some may not understand, but friends will or at least the friends you need will. Some may think you are too intense, but when they see the fruit of your vision on the other side, they will understand and not only that, they will be encouraged and inspired. In fact, I kindly requested the nurses and doctors no longer enter my room except as medically needed. I quite literally shut the door! Pretty bold a move from someone stuck in the hospital. Having their attention was kind of the point. But I had all of the reports I needed, and I couldn't afford anything or anyone speaking contrary, believing contrary or even looking contrary to the vision of victory and success I had in my mind and heart. I had to birth a miracle!

What's that miracle of a vision inside of you? That too big for human hands kind of vision? That vision that has God's name written all over it? I, as will you, had to stay seated in mind and spirit in a place above my limited resources, above my daunting circumstances and above what seemed impossible. And yes, folks thought I lost my marbles. Soon the hospital's social worker showed up, and I realized this sweet lady thought I was losing my right mind. Bless her heart, but I had to kindly ask her to leave too! It's funny to think about in reflection but at the time, I was sweating, I was pushing, and the situation was critical. When you too grasp the power of vision and what it can do to push you to the other side of your greatness and into your next level purposes, you too will be equality protective and unapologetic.

But it's not enough to talk about the power of vision. Let me demonstrate it. Once I created a room with God in my place of solitude to secure clarity and assurance on the vision for our lives, it pushed my faith into realms that truly helped manifest the miracles. And let me be clear, I sought God's vision, not my own desires. I asked Him to prepare my heart and see Him in the midst of loss if that was part of our journey. But instead, He uncovered in our case a "gut" knowing that this sickness was not unto death for us. He reminded me of the prophecy in our baby's name that He uploaded in advance to give direction, and He prepared me with a knowing that it would get worse before it got better. But in the end, I knew that we would surely speak of and exemplify His glory.

The faithful morning that Legend was born, they had to pump my body with over two people's worth of blood to try to keep me alive, my lungs collapsed during the surgery and delivery, I had so much vascular trauma my blood pressure was through the roof and I lost so much blood and platelets that once the delivery and surgeries where complete, my blood would not coagulate, or clot. But here is to the power of a deep-seated vision. While recovering in ICU, there was a time that I didn't fully understand while there, but I only recalled that I was desperate to tell my husband David, "No!" I couldn't speak, I couldn't move, I was just frustrated and desperate to get that simple but clearly important message to him. It was like a dream, but then again it wasn't. Weeks later, I was able to put it all together when one of our friends who was in my ICU room with me after Legend's delivery shared that the doctor came into the room and told David that he should probably contact my parents and additional loved ones because if I "didn't turn the corner soon, I wouldn't make it". She shared with me that I was sedated at the time and for all they knew, I was resting and unaware. But in response to what the doctor said, I suddenly began to try to move and actually shook my head from left to right, to respond with a clear and adamant, "No!" They were all shocked and so was I when she shared the story. Vision was so deep in my spirit that death could not have me! My spirit took over when my mind and body couldn't. That's what vision, deep-rooted, incubated vision will do for you! It will protect your atmosphere and war after the inheritance of your vision when you get a hold of it. It will help you fight with resilience and tenacity you didn't know you had when you are empowered by vision. Several days later before I was released from ICU, I noticed the doctor was staring

> **It will help you fight with resilience and tenacity you didn't know you had when you are empowered by vision.**

at me from outside the room. He finally came in and explained to me how grave my circumstances were and that he was literally in awe that I was still alive. And then he said words with a felt conviction that still ring clear as a bell in my mind even as I write, "Surely, God is on your side." Yes, indeed!

Know this, when you are motivated by and committed to your God inspired vision, your outcomes will speak to the glory of God that is with you, and you will provide hope to those you don't even know are watching.

When you invest your time, heart and spirit to the cause of vision in the 360 areas of your life, wisdom, provision, and direction will even flow to you in alignment with the vision. God will not inspire a vision for which he has not already made a way. I was too sick to visit Legend in the neonatal intensive care unit at first and spent several days in ICU after his birth myself. It took several more days for me to be released from the hospital and quite some time for me to be well enough to regularly visit Legend and his 1 pound self, connected to monitors and wires from every which way possible. But vision gave me wisdom beyond myself, and I knew I had to create the same environment for Legend that I created for myself although I couldn't physically be with him. I helped him line up his mind, heart, and spirit with the vision. I was a worship leader at the time and Wisdom inspired me to record my voice on tape capturing worship and a place of anointing through song. I spoke and sang to Legend's entire body, his collapsed lungs, his septic blood, immature eyes, his at-risk brain… "I command your mind to praise the Lord, I command your mind to praise the Lord!" "I command your lungs to praise the Lord, I command your lungs to praise the Lord!" "I command your eyes, to praise the Lord, I command your eyes, to praise the Lord!"

I recorded words I believed were from heaven for him to hear. That his name was Legend and that God named him "one who inspires." I left him with the words of encouragement and love he was used to everyday while he was in my belly. I poured over his environment scripture that lined up with the vision

And he heard all of this every single day.

I saw for him. And he heard all of this every single day. He then lived through the most critical initial days. Soon, he was off the respirator, and we were finally able to hold him. Then he was eating on his own and without tubes. And the next thing we knew he was released to go home an entire month before expected. He was still only 4 pounds 9 ounces at that time and way too little for me to feel comfortable about it all, but he was simply too healthy to remain in the hospital. His will was empowered and determined to align with the vision that was planted in his environment, and he left impossible in the wind. Figuring out how to change that little diaper, hold that little body and having him home sooner than we imagined was a good problem to have.

Vision injects unshakeable faith into our journey, aligns our actions and motivations to our determined ends, inspires wisdom and insight beyond ourselves and helps us give birth to outcomes that are beyond our sight and are in sync with an extraordinary God.

So then, I hope you see without a doubt that the rewards are golden to shutting the door and creating room for God in a place of reflection and surrender in order to uncover with clarity the visions in our hearts.

What does this precious time look like?

Your time in incubating vision is an intentional time in which you remove distractions and create room for reflection, prayer and putting your inspired thoughts together. Whether a weekend or a week, just remember that God's voice is louder the more quiet time we spend with Him. Now for some, this time of solitude may even be a season. And perhaps it happens to be the season you are in as you are reading this book. So if that is you, don't be dismayed at the friends you have lost in your season, the seemingly lonely journey you may be

Your time in incubating vision is an intentional time.

experiencing and the change of pace that has shifted in your life. These seasons, as uncomfortable as they might be, are the ripe ones for fresh vision to be uncovered or clarified with brilliance you might, otherwise, miss. So trust God in your process and utilize your time well to pray the questions you have been carrying, search your heart for inspiration, journal, and process what God is speaking to you. It's important enough a vision to God's Kingdom plan that He personally set your birthing room in order to help you shift your heart and motivations to align with your next season. So honor it, saturate your mind with His word and up-level how you direct your attention towards the Father. To whom much is given, much is required.[12] So know that the discipline you gain during this time is only an investment to your being sustained in your next level journey.

Your seeking during this time is also active and alive. Like king Jehoshaphat, it may look like a time of fasting for you should you be so inspired. Fasting helps you posture yourself in a spirit of surrender; it helps you purify the distractions within, and is a commitment to

---

[12] Luke 12:48

51

your place of humility in seeking the almighty voice and presence of God as your source of inspiration. I personally find fasting to be an integral part of my vision casting process and commit to a fast annually for that purpose as I evaluate and align and then fast additionally as the spirit leads. This time should also certainly be a time of prayer and talking with God

Fasting helps you posture yourself in a spirit of surrender.

as you allow space to simply rest in His presence while actively journaling and processing your thoughts and dreams. (Returning to your vision prompts and reflections will be a valuable tool for you here.) It should be a time of delighting in God such as through the study of scripture, listening to Bible-based teachings and sermons daily, and setting an atmosphere in which He can rest richly with you. And it may even be a time of connecting with a trusted mentor or life coach to help you walk through your time of seeking and gaining greater awareness of what's in your heart.

As you have been able to see, shutting the door, delighting yourself in the Lord and investing time in uncovering God inspired vision and in other cases maintaining that vision is how you set the stage to give birth to vision and manifest your re-imagined life with outcomes that are beautifully, brilliantly and powerfully God.

CHAPTER 6

Vision Strategy #3
Push

"I advise you to say your dream is possible and then overcome all inconveniences, ignore all the hassles and take a running leap through the hoop, even if it is in flames."

-LES BROWN

There are times in our lives when we operate in the greatest wisdom by embracing stillness. That can be the case when we are seeking *revelation* of vision. But when it comes to cooperating with the *manifestation* of our visions, we have got to be disciplined, diligent, and doggedly determined. In fact, as natural a response as it may seem, there is no real value in even

> When it comes to cooperating with the manifestation of our visions, we have got to be disciplined, diligent, and doggedly determined.

examining the cost when you know your vision is a God inspired one. The commitment is about the steps directed towards your destiny rather than your preoccupation with the process. You have simply got to push! The greatness, the fulfillment, the impact, the authority, the liberty, the joy, the restoration, the legacy and the testimony on the other side are worth it. You are worth it!

Your strategy to "push" means being willing to become comfortable with being uncomfortable, to do what others may not be willing to do, and to take little care for how your wholehearted commitment may be perceived in the midst of it. The truth is that sometimes your push just ain't pretty. Oh but the blessing on the other side indeed is!

Obedience and Protection

Perhaps you grew up like me with a mama who was incredibly big on love but who didn't have room for a few things and one of them was a little girl "being grown." I knew better than to have mama give a direction and then ask, "Well, Why?" even if a sincere ask. There was just something about a grown person having to explain themselves and a child simply not moving in obedience as a response. That was just not an acceptable combination. The likely answer "in my day" was something like; "Because I said so!" It's a funny memory and perhaps shared by many. We knew that when you get a direction, especially from your mama, the expected response was simply to obediently comply.

So remember my mama when it comes to "gut" directions and promptings from the Holy Spirit as you push towards the manifestation of your vision. This too is just one time when you need to respond and move with swift obedience simply because God said so. You may not always understand the why and you may not always be able to handle the why. But when you know you are being inspired towards action don't get paralyzed as you analyze, or make procrastination your habit, move and act in alignment with God's voice because even seemingly simple inspirations can carry significant weight by protecting outcomes aligned with your purpose.

I would never have imagined that a simple inspiration to wake up early each day would have been the difference between life and death for Legend and me. But as I continued to place the vision before God, pray about and ask for His guidance, strength, and insight, I knew I had to work my life like a winner. I knew I had to train my body to operate in the present like it would need to successfully operate in the future time of the manifestation of the vision. I was already a mother of a toddler, a wife, and with a career waiting in the balance. With a newborn to be added to the mix, I then began to prepare my body for the 5:00 am mornings that I knew I would need to manage with an expanding family and the complete vision I had before me. The nurses loved me because they just thought I was an early riser so they could count on visiting and beginning their rounds early with me each day.

But the truth was, I was working my vision. God gave me that simple instruction- to wake at 5:00 am. I even used arm weights during that time to exercise my arm muscles since my muscles were growing

I was singularly focused on simply aligning my present disciplines to match the order I would need at the point of manifestation.

weak from the prolonged bed rest. I was preparing my arms to hold the weight of the vision, our baby, despite every idea and diagnosis otherwise. I was postured in my push! I was diligent in the details and did what I was inspired to do without asking a lot of questions. I didn't care how crazy I looked. I was singularly focused on simply aligning my present disciplines to match the order I would need at the point of manifestation. That is a demonstration of your push.

As it would be, that obedience was protection. At exactly 6:00 am on November 24, 2008, the hemorrhage "event" happened. I was thoroughly schooled by the doctors and team. And our plan was rehearsed a dozen times, so I knew exactly what to expect and how to discern should this dreaded event happen. And when it did, it was beyond comprehensible.

"Stat!"...I looked to the left of me as the nurses were feverishly moving about and preparing me for delivery and it was as if someone had poured an entire red bucket of paint beside me. It was unbelievable. Things were grim in minutes. I looked up and saw the lead nurse with whom I had gathered all types of recipes and stories by this time into my hospital stay as she moved about with tears in her eyes. I knew what she was thinking, and I just began to pray in the spirit. I prayed for my husband, my boys and for me as I listened to them coordinate the fastest route to the surgical unit in this quite moderately sized Nashville hospital. We weren't in Chicago or New York where such a plan might seem worthy, but it was just one more indication that there was not even a second to lose.

But the power is in the details! Oh, the divine and Master-full set up on this journey. The fact is, this all-important, life-threatening, purpose defeating event began at exactly 6:00 a.m. Rather than me promptly alerting the nurses because I was alert and awake at 5:00 as God directed, it could have all very easily happened in my sleep and unbeknownst to me. Without that simple, **It took discipline.** but significant, offering of faith and obedience it could have been a much more tragic outcome. Critical moments would have been lost with the medical team most likely finding me and likely finding me too late. This "event" is painless; there are really no signs that might surely wake up a mother who is sound asleep when it happens. But God knew in advance the ambush that was orchestrated ahead, and he set me up strategically for the win. I was awake, alert, in position and prepared. It took discipline; there was no one else to which I could be accountable but God, no one was forcing me to wake up daily like a mother of two. But rather it was the dogged determination to see this vision through as my offering in my push to the manifestation.

Dear sister, hear me and please hear me well. If God is telling you to seek out a location, seek out a location. If He is telling you to invest more significantly in your health, invest in your health. If He is telling you to get more training, get more training. If He is telling you to pray more consistently, pray more consistently. If He tells you to stand on your head at noon each day, stand on your head at noon each day…well you get the picture. The point is that *whatever* you are getting a Holy Spirit nudge to do, even if it seems out of time, out of place or unimportant, do it and do it with all diligence. You can be setting a path for your preparation to meet opportunity and collide for tremendous success at the right time. Know that your commitment to push in your birthing room-the time, the obedience and the discipline you offer- can give life to your vision and protect precious outcomes that you would have never contemplated.

~Hit Replay~

Uncovering vision gives power. Maintaining vision is your superpower. It is one thing for us to have the empowered edge of a vision. But it is a next-level strategy for us to commit to maintaining that vision before us daily. Life, challenges, distraction, busyness, detours, and setbacks have cunning ways of getting us off track. So

Our job is to be as preoccupied with our purposes as the enemy.

your posture to "push" once you have uncovered vision for your life must also include your commitment to keep that vision before you. Our job is to be as preoccupied with our purposes as the enemy. We don't get a day off!

Clearly, I had set a precedent for going rogue at this point. Keeping doctors and staff out of my hospital room and such. So in like fashion, I took to decorate the walls of my hospital room which was now my second home. You can laugh here, don't worry, I didn't really. But I did ask my husband to enlarge this powerful prayer of protection and success in pregnancy which directly spoke to the vision I had in my heart that a dear friend sent to me. I asked that he get it enlarged as big as possible, where I could actually read each word on the wall from my bed and anyone who entered could do the same. My strategy was not only to keep the vision in my face daily, but I knew that every doctor and every nurse couldn't help but read this "in your face" declaration too. I was not short on exceptional care by our team of nurses and doctors, but this was a move to help remind even their thoughts and hopes of the God in whom we were relying and to get every critical person on board and in agreement. There were times when staff would even take a moment and read before they left the room which was no doubt significant re-alignment from the frequent detours and setbacks that were coming our way. You must be disciplined, diligent, and doggedly determined.

Whether at work, at church, or with your family at home, making the vision plain so that anyone who reads it can faithfully and easily align is critical in your "push."[13] To set the vision once is not enough. You must rehearse that vision like a Broadway production! They rehearse 7 hours a day for six days a week by the way.[14] An intense rehearsal schedule for immensely powerful outcomes. Whether your vision is written, it is in the form of pictures on your vision boards or spoken as your daily affirmations (I do all three!), you must hit replay daily so that the adventure of life and all of its twists and turns do not snuff life out of your visions. This is a critical part of your push.

> **You must rehearse that vision like a Broadway production!**

Then the LORD said to me, "Write my answer plainly on tablets so that a runner can carry the correct message to others. Habakkuk 2:2 NLT

I recently saw a precious example of this in my home, and it was actually through Legend. As a family we continue to live out what God has revealed through this journey and not only do I personally create

---

[13] inspired by Habakkuk 2:0

[14] http://www.playbill.com/article/ask-playbillcom-rehearsal-schedule-com-146459

my own vision statements and take great care in creating visions boards that are visible throughout my office and home, but we also create vision boards and statements as a family. During the summer, the boys create a vision board of top goals they want to accomplish over the summer as well as at the top of the school year. As a family, we have vision boards, and a favorite one is of our next home. One day, Legend walked into the room, stood in front of that vision board, he looked up, down, side to side, took it all in and walked back out. He often does that. I then heard him tell his brothers, "Our next home will…"

It's as good as done in his heart and mind. Rehearsing your vision and creating your vision statements/boards of what God inspires from

We have got to be disciplined, diligent, and doggedly determined.

your heart not only keeps your faith and focus sure, but it also directs the focus and belief of your teams, your families, your churches and your groups. We have got to be disciplined, diligent, and doggedly determined. We've got to push!

Divine Empowerment

As we wrap up our time together in this section "Giving Birth To Vision" and our three areas of focus (Listen to your heart, Shut the Door, and Push), I first want to thank you for allowing me to share this deeply personal story with you. I pray that as you have seen the faithfulness of God in our lives and the principles of vision God uncovered through our journey, that your lives are not only impacted but also transformed at the heart level in how you will strategize and operate in the strength of your re-imagined lives. Truly "with God all things are possible."[15] But secondly, it's equally important for you to take with you the fact that there was no step taken, no revelation had, and no deep-seated discipline employed without what I clearly recognized to be a divine empowerment. I love this exchange in scripture between God and this wise father in verses Mark 9:23-24 (NLT):

"What do you mean, 'If I can'?" Jesus asked. "Anything is possible if a person believes. The father instantly cried out, "I do believe, but help me overcome my unbelief!"

Sometimes we alone are simply not enough. We believe in Jesus the Christ, and we believe that he is able but we still need help to overcome our unbelief. We may be called to higher levels of discipline and we may even have some measure of discipline to work with but may still need help with more as we push to the vision. Listen, I have not shared with you the story of a woman with super human faith, or super human discipline or super human ability. I shared with you the story of a woman who looked to a God with super human faith, super human discipline and super human ability to empower me to operate

---

[15] Matthew 9:26

in elevated realms of belief and action to uncover and manifest vision. It is Ok for God to inspire a direction and for you to still look to him for the strength to align with that direction. He is ever after your dependence and heart in this journey,

He is ever after your dependence and heart in this journey,

and He will supply your every need for the vision. You will never be called to a place where supply is lacking. Just look to Jesus in every step of the way like a baby looks to its mother for supply for surely *He who promised is faithful.*[16]

---

[16] Hebrews 10:23

PART 2

LIFE RE-IMAGINED
~THE MINDSET~

3 Key Mindset Strategies

"Little girls with dreams become women with vision."

-AUTHOR UNKNOWN

THE RE-IMAGINED LIFE: INTRODUCTION

Beautifully Evolved

"Evolve into the complete person you were intended to be."

OPRAH WINFREY

I pray you have been able to take in with fresh eyes and a renewed sense of consciousness the power that vision has on our lives, our sense of fulfillment and our motivation towards purposeful and powerful ends. As we now zoom in our discussion to specifically touch on the "Re-Imagined life" and how it builds upon vision to take shape, our theme shifts to embracing and recognizing as women how over time and seasons we are wonderfully and beautifully evolved all the more for God's work and His glory. The re-imagined life takes vision as a necessary foundation and infuses it with a relevant sense of vibrancy by acknowledging and embracing the gift of our evolution.

The re-imagined life invites that evolution to help us refresh the screens of our vision as we move in and out of seasons. As we evolve, grow, mature and shift, so too should our God inspired visions just enough to refresh and align them with how God has evolved our lives and capacity in time. As God takes us personally to the next levels of growth and ability, so too, we must revisit and refine our vision to uncover that complimentary next level dream. That's a "life re-imagined" lifestyle.

Since the third grade, I have known nothing but glasses and four eyes. My strawberry shortcake glasses and first pair of specs no doubt saved the day. I have "near-sighted" vision. Essentially, that means that I have to be closer to things to see the details more clearly. Sure I see there is a sign on the door, but I might not be able to make out what it says until I am much closer. So too, when it comes to our visions, sometimes the fine details are much clearer to make out the further along we are in our lives, and the more we grow and evolve with each step forward to the next door through which we may shift or upgrade our position.

As we commit to making the shifts that this book talks about, especially in moving from frustrated to fulfilled, it's important to lay hold of the empowering fact that being out of sync and not honoring our beautifully evolved lives in the lifetime of our vision can also be the cause of us feeling discontented, unfulfilled, trapped by limitations and misaligned. I call it a spiritual wedgie. Yes, just pretty dog on uncomfortable until you do something about it.

And it was that level of disconnect between my own evolution and my vision that pushed me into my re-imagined life for this season. That helped this attorney and mediator re-imagine and shift into a life of greater fulfillment, alignment, satisfaction and impact as a life and leadership/executive coach, speaker and entrepreneur with some acting and modeling mixed in there too! Life now is like Oprah Winfrey's treasured Christmas tradition-a mix of all my "favorite things." It's an adventure, and I am faithfully and thoroughly enjoying the ride. But escaping the confines of comfort definitely took some internal work through an imperfectly perfect process from which I can now glean wisdom to help support the push of others like you to their re-imagined success.

On the surface, it may appear a complete metamorphosis, but it really was shifting the emphasis of the gifts I already had while honoring convictions that evolved over time. And so it's important to know that your re-imagined life is not necessarily about a big, dramatic shift, although it very well may be a reinvention of sorts for some as it was

Taking the time to re-align will help you operate at greater levels of satisfaction.

for me. But know also that as you take queues to reimagine your life to a greater place of fulfillment and update the vision, it may simply be more of an important revision and tweak to honor your growth and the evolved insight, values and circumstances of your current season. Regardless of how significant the shift, taking the time to re-align will help you operate at greater levels of satisfaction.

There was a time I will admit that I couldn't quite relate to the idea of purposefully leaving my career and staying home for a season as a mother because the desire was still remote for me. But in this season my re-imagined life is very much inspired by how I build my career around a greater level of flexibility and availability specifically for my children and family. Entrepreneurship was in the

> **As women and life bearers we are born and intended to reflect a shine that is luminous and energetic.**

vision, but it wasn't until later that I could see it was "the" vision for this season. My heart for walking alongside women was always there and expressed but had shifted to a full-blown passion and to the forefront as well did the weight of my experiences, maturity, training, and journey. But here is the deal. Even with all of that, it would have been very possible to have these resounding shifts take place in my life and still stay

> **We have to make shifts in our mentality before we can see a different reality.**

parked in a place where I was discontented, frustrated, under utilized, under recognized and unmotivated. Or even to be moderately satisfied, moderately challenged and moderately motivated is not enough. As women and life bearers we are born and intended to reflect a shine that is luminous and energetic. The truth is that it is easier, much easier, to live in the comfort of what we know and what we can control than take the risk and muster the courage to make the shifts that are speaking to us when its time to re-imagine and up-level our dream. We have to make shifts in our mentality before we can see a different reality.

Signals to Shift

Just like we need and have traffic signals to help control the flow and help us shift at major points of intersection, we too have signals in our lives to help us slow down, pause and shift our direction at significant points of intersection in our journeys. A prominent signal is in times of transition and change. More often we find that transition rest on the backside of seasons of evolution or are a part of our evolution. That evolution may be in the way of our circumstances, our mindsets, our desires, our maturity, our skillsets and the like. And transition can signal and squeeze us to align our flow and direction with our new ways of thinking, being and living. If you don't listen, you may be nudged by a mighty uncomfortable spiritual wedgie that you can't ignore like I was, so dear friends, pay attention! But seriously, as you renew your experience towards a most fulfilling, purposeful and vibrant experience through a re-imagined lifestyle, a strong signal to help you evaluate your flow, take stock of your evolution and perhaps shift lanes in your journey to your destination is when you sense transition and significant change in your life. Your presence is evolving and its time to re-visit the vision to access, re-align and fine tune.

Re-Imagination Inspiration

A popular motivation I've shared over time is "Dream like a girl, but war like a woman!" It seems to really resonate, and I'm glad it does because if I were to sum up both the

"Dream like a girl, but war like a woman!"

motivation you need to re-imagine your life and the inspiration from which you would draw from, it would be wrapped up in this tiny 7-word package. You must be motivated with a warrior princess like tenacity towards the beautiful, liberating and aspirational end that captures the fearlessness and limitless boundaries of your childhood imagination. Life has a way of burying dreams that were once purely inspired by your heart and unique design. In fact, when you begin to walk through the 360-vision guide I've developed for you, you will find that I may encourage you from time to time to explore within that exercise thoughts which you might have had with regards to a certain area of vision when you were a young girl.

Connecting you to the girl inside of you is strategic and an important part of being courageously authentic in re-imagining your vision and tapping into places of joy and fulfillment that are still longing for re-connection. Little you was actually pretty big and bold!

She wasn't scarred by failures, missteps, disappointments, and let-downs. She dreamed authentically, hopefully, naively and without hindrance. She didn't know the cost; she just knew what her heartfelt. As you begin to put together the visions God has for you, listen to her and acknowledge her as you begin to build upon and uncover with greater clarity what's presently speaking from your heart.

Little you was actually pretty big and bold!

When I was a young girl, I used to wrap one of my night gowns around my head (that was my long voluminous hair), get in front of the mirror and go to town singing Diana Ross for my pretend audience. I was always singing, I later jumped into the pageant scene, and I loved the challenge of theater. But as I matured, and had to examine why those dreams were still relevant for me in some way at this point in my journey, I also began to understand that as I have evolved that a big part of that draw at present was not only my love for the arts and the stage but the appreciation I had for the platform it provides to further express good and inspire.

But friend, by the time I finished law school and had enough of life under my belt, I also had enough failures, flops, crazy messages and frustrations that stifled my courage to wholeheartedly express those talents and pursue those visions. I eventually took the safe route. And guess what, even in my successes, I carried some level of nagging frustration. But I am grateful God was developing a

Visions and desires inspired by a limitless God don't expire.

bigger story. A message that it is never too late and that visions and desires inspired by a limitless God don't expire. That if you trust God and muster the courage to re-imagine your life and pull up inspirations from your most authentic design and heartfelt desires, that He will meet your courage as a redeemer of time. It can even be a richer journey for having reclaimed your dream and committed against all odds to nourish it.

So the beauty of today is that I have begun to recapture those visions through the power of re-imagination, but it is now an even more colorful tapestry with my family and kids a part of that picture.

Rather than the vision I saw as a young girl which only involved me in that picture, in my evolved season as a wife and mother, I have captured the beauty and order set by this season and blended that into this re-imagined dream. And so it is that now my sons and I enjoy acting and modeling together, we grow together, we find a place to encourage others young and old together, and we learn about business and building their little brands together. And through this re-imagined vision, their involvement is just one way that as a mother I can help them learn to stretch to see and believe in bigger God-sized possibilities as a matter of course. So we are also building our belief muscles together.

Certainly, a far richer and rewarding experience than I first imagined and which would have never been actualized without the power of re-imagination at work and the inspirations of little Keitra influencing my heart. Reimagining your life requires that as a part of that process you consider those imaginations that once purely influenced your dreams and pay attention to whether they are still speaking to you as you evolve and align. You must "dream like a child, but war like a woman"!

With this introduction to what it means to tap into your "re-imagined" lifestyle and vision, in the pages ahead, the goal is to help equip you with key strategies to support your success in making the necessary shifts in your mindset because without a doubt that's really where the Re-Imagined shift begins and ends... in your mind.

CHAPTER 7

Mindset Strategy #1
Mental Fortitude

"When anyone tells me I can't do anything... I'm just not listening anymore."

-FLORENCE GRIFFITH JOYNER, "FLO-JO"
THE WORLDS FASTEST WOMEN"

Growing up I remember this absolutely gorgeous woman, whose strength shown with every powerful stride she made on the track. Her hair flowed behind her with elegance, and her six inch adorned nails were not only the talk of many but further solidified her display of what unconventional and regal looked like together. She was one-of-a-kind and was none other than Florence Griffith Joyner, known to most as "Flo-Jo." Flo Jo's power, the immaculate form of her athletic body, and her trademark position as the "The World's Fastest Woman" left lasting impressions on the world as well as this impressionable teenage girl. But perhaps the most outstanding inspiration from this African American woman world athlete from the projects of South Central Los Angeles was a story she shared of her commitment to her vision of becoming a world top athlete. She explained that she knew she had to win first in her mind, so she read this one motivational book over and over and over again until it literally began to fall apart. She kept it held together by rubber bands. She knew intuitively even at a young age that she had to be an Olympian in her mind first before she was an Olympian in fact. Flo-Jo conquered every limiting factor in her mind first to go on to make her mark as not only a world record holder twice over, but fashion designer, actress, writer, sports caster and co-chair of the President's Council on Physical Fitness and Sports.[17]

Aligning with the greatness inside of each of us and making moves to shift to align more directly with our heart's vision can be tough work. Many people and things may get in our way, but what will really cause a visionary to stall is what we let get or stay in our heads, and Flo-Jo knew that. Your mental fortitude of which we speak here relates to your thought life.

Now I'll be honest, re-imagining your life can be scary. You may have to take risk to align your evolved self with the next level of your vision that may pull you out of your comfort zone. You may have to let go of some things that no longer belong, but that are still what you

---

[17] http://www.florencegriffithjoyner.com/index.html

know and what you know well. You may have to take a pay cut in your check before you are the one cutting the checks. It's a process, and you can get disillusioned if in advance you don't gear up like the champion that you are and build your mind for your designed victory.

Wherefore gird up the loins of your mind, be sober, and hope to the end for the grace that is to be brought unto you at the revelation of Jesus Christ;
1 Peter 1:13 KJV

This scripture is power packed with strategy particularly as we examine the need for mental fortitude. This verse hits square on with the weight our minds and thought life carry. The scripture shares that we are to gird or protect the "loins" of our minds. The loins are areas of reproduction. It is one thing to be diligent and protect the thoughts of our minds, and it is entirely another to be diligent to protect what our minds reproduce. The anatomy of your mind is equipped to duplicate and reproduce thought. If you let in thoughts like ones that you are not good enough, smart enough, or ready enough, that is what will be reproduced in your mind and ultimately what it is you believe. One thought is as a hundred and in building your mental fortitude, you have to arrest every thought that is not built in the authority, ability, provision and revelation of Christ as you re-imagine your life.

Like Flo-Jo, we have to rehearse the pages of the book of possibility in our minds until the pages fall apart because as you do, you begin to train that muscle of your mind to leap over hurdles that are planted by fear and illusion. The affirmations you generate through your self-coaching guide in this book can be a good part of that regime with revisions made as you see needed in order to re-imagine along the way. To every action, there is an equal and opposite reaction, and you must fortify your mind at every opportunity to counter thoughts of impossibility and fear with thoughts of possibility and faith. This isn't something you do on occasion, it must be an active, *daily* exercise to fortify and affirm your mind with the language of possibility.

~Courage~

Also in the way of mental fortitude is the need to be women of courage as we live out our re-imagined lifestyles. Not everyone is willing to do what it takes to get the outcomes that you see for yourself in your heart, so the road less traveled can be lonely and lightly affirmed. No one who loves you wants to see you flop. So where your shift requires a leap, not everyone may be able to affirm your conviction for fear you may stumble. And the truth is, even if you do, you are stumbling forward and in the direction of something greater! Even our flops can fuel us forward and teach us lessons on the road to greater. It takes courage to trust God calling you to more or different and to trust him alone or with a limited fan base. And that's ok when we are divinely motivated and not spitefully so to prove our point because this isn't about simply existing and being, this is about tapping into a life that is fully you, fully God and fully purposeful all at the same time. That is a pretty sweet spot worth a temporary press to shift and align.

> 1Then the LORD spoke to Moses saying, 2"Send out for yourself men so that they may spy out the land of Canaan, which I am going to give to the sons of Israel;…30Then Caleb quieted the people before Moses and said, "We should by all means go up and take possession of it, for we will surely overcome it." 31But the men who had gone up with him said, "We are not able to go up against the people, for they are too strong for us." 32So they gave out to the sons of Israel a bad report of the land which they had spied out, saying, "The land through which we have gone, in spying it out, is a land that devours its inhabitants; and all the people whom we saw in it are men of *great* size. 33"There also we saw the Nephilim (the sons of Anak are part of the Nephilim); and we became like grasshoppers in our own sight, and so we were in their sight."
> Numbers 13:1-2, 30-33 NASB

Many are familiar with this passage of scripture where Moses sends spies to check out the land they are to possess. There is no question here on what the vision for the people of God is because God made it quite clear and told Moses that this was the land that He would give to them. So the spies peeped out what it would take to get there and obtain the vision, and somehow Caleb returned with a belief that no one other person who also checked out the same land and inhabitants had. He was more than courageous, Caleb was unshakeable. He shut down the naysayers. He alone had the courage to believe that they were *more* than able to take on the giants in the land and boldly quieted the voices of everyone else who believed it an impossible and unlikely win. They all saw the same thing, but only he had the courage to believe. And so it is that unlike all of the others who were with him, he indeed did inherit and walk into his promised land. The question is will you forfeit what God is showing you is already yours or will you take hold of courage, wear it with strength and shut down the voice of fear and doubt when it speaks?

Courage will take you places that others aren't willing to go both literally and in faith. You must harness the courage to make moves outside of your comfort level and often times outside of the comfort level of your tribe. But like Caleb, it starts with a fortified mind and sure resolves that if God said it, then I am "more than able" to win.

~Identification Realignment~

"Challenges are gifts that force us to search for a new center of gravity. Don't fight them. Just find a new way to stand."

— OPRAH WINFREY

79

As you begin to make courageous moves and master the discipline to gird your mind with strategic thoughts, the final focus in the way of mental fortitude that I wish to make sure you embrace is making room for identification realignment. This is more of an awareness step than it is an action step because just by giving yourself the space to expect a bit of turbulence in the process of repositioning yourself with your realigned vision, you will enforce your footing as you adjust and evolve.

As you re-imagine your life and fine-tune your vision and journey towards it, you may find that a fresh look at your most authentic self in this season looks different than the woman you have known for a while. Your refreshed vision may shift you into new arenas, spheres of influence, relationships, careers or simply alter the way you deliver your gifts and talents to others. Simply put, it may take some time to recognize yourself in the mirror after your make-over. You may look absolutely stunning, but you may look different. It's important to know as you align and re-imagine that it is fair and appropriate for **That re-imagined woman deserves your grace.** your equilibrium to be challenged as you find your center of gravity in discovering your footing in your shift. There is no perfect or right way to it. You just have to dig in, make the shifts, and be kind enough to yourself to allow for rediscovery as you adjust to your refreshed view. It is not very different from a new job or position where you are given grace and an initial time to acclimate yourself to all that is new to you. So as you take leaps to new levels of your evolved journey and honor your beautifully evolved self in the re-imagination process, give yourself some room and embrace the fact that that repositioning yourself may be perfectly imperfect a process. We women can be terribly hard on ourselves, so this discussion is an important, and, I hope, a liberating one. That re-imagined woman deserves your grace.

I can share this wisdom with you with such a heartfelt degree of compassion because I know first hand how disorienting it can be as you muster the courage to soar just a little bit higher and in alignment with where your journey is calling you. I had losses before I had gains, I sank before I swam, and I crawled before I learned to walk. But, I got to that re-imagined place I could see for this new season of my life. I did have something that I have now shared with you and with which you are now equally empowered, and that is a deeply overcoming reference point- my testimony of a limitless and consistent God. This surely empowered my perspective and helped me realize that the

The challenges of one's journey do not forfeit the manifestation of their destiny.

challenges of one's journey do not forfeit the manifestation of their destiny. I had already experienced what it was like for things to get worse before they got better and that still have no effect whatsoever on the promise and vision of God in my life. So sister, as you shift and take hold of your next level of vision, learn, figure out, grow from your losses, celebrate the gains and just be sure to keep on moving. You *will* gain your equilibrium, move past the atmospheric turbulence and soar in your re-imagined view. If you maintain your faith and keep moving, you most assuredly will.

CHAPTER 8

Key Mindset Strategy #2
You Are Worthy

You don't give yourself enough credit. I believe in you.

-JUDY MUSGRAVE, MY MOTHER

Oh if you ever need a good dose of the truth, you just ask my mama, Mrs. Judy. She is a mom to many and doesn't mind telling the truth because she will fight for the best in you. She is overflowing with love and wisdom that speaks volumes. So I thought no better way to begin this chapter than with words from Mama Judy to you. Because this is a place where you have to make some clear and intentional heart and mind connections. These are words she has shared with me that I still pull up from time to time to remind myself of what's in me. These words speak to the significant mental posture we must own when we upgrade our visions at evolved stages

> You can absolutely limit your ability to even see your re-imagined self if you don't recognize the depth of your worth.

and align our reimagined lives. You can absolutely limit your ability to even see your re-imagined self if you don't recognize the depth of your worth.

Becoming Self-aware

Feelings of unworthiness are tricky. They hide in a lack of self-confidence that isn't always apparent to us. When you are stretching yourself to some place you have never been, you can easily question your qualifications. All the more, when you are stretching your mind to *imagine* yourself someplace you have never been, you can easily question your qualifications. Tapping into your worthiness for your God inspired visions requires a keen sense of awareness.

Are you shortchanging the trajectory of your vision for feeling unworthy of a higher destination?

Are you shortchanging the trajectory of your vision for feeling unworthy of a higher destination? Sometimes we just aren't as aware of our self-limiting beliefs as we thought. And now is a good time to begin to be clearer and more honest with those areas where our confidence is lacking and may cause us to feel that we don't deserve what God has for us.

It is much easier for us to see the next level success of someone else and think that absolutely makes sense for them and not ourselves because then we have to take responsibility and own it. We have to do the work to dig down deep, increase our belief system and stretch our level of trust in ourselves and in our God. When you consider the vision that is forming for you, before settling with it, be sure to ask yourself and consider these 2 questions: 1) What would an even bigger picture look like? 2) What is it that is keeping me from thinking and believing that bigger picture is the vision for me?

~

You too are worthy
You too are worthy to live that way, you are worthy to give that way, you are worthy to own that way, you are worthy to love that way, you are worthy to lead that way, you are worthy to be free that way, you are worthy to serve that way, you are worthy to succeed that way
You too are worthy

~

As you look to gain a heightened sense of awareness of what it is you believe about yourself, I also encourage you to examine those places where your emotions and character may be misaligned. For example, be mindful of places where as a woman of light you feel or hear a story of success and feel resentful in some way in response. Be mindful of places as a woman of light where you internally shut down opportunities to celebrate other's successes. Be mindful of places, as a woman of light, where there is an opportunity presented to you, which will align with your desires and the outcomes of your vision, but the only thing keeping you from moving forward is whether or not you are capable of succeeding. Those examples are good places to trigger you to examine if your confidence or lack of it is being confronting and even more specifically if you are being challenged to own your sense of worthiness and your seat at the table.

Not believing you are worthy can keep you repeating patterns that are beneath your great place. I may not know you personally, and we may have never met or talked one-on-one, but I would venture to say that Mama Judy's words to me are equally relevant to you as well. I'm going out on a limb and pretty confident you probably don't give yourself all the credit you deserve. Particularly as women, it is much easier to identify what we are not than celebrate what we are. This instinct also causes many of us to be much more likely to hold on to past failures as a bar to our success and how we evaluate our worth. In fact, a Harvard Business review study of more than 10,000 executives found that women were more than 1.5 times as likely as men to not even apply for senior executive level positions if they had earlier been rejected for a role.[18] Listen, comebacks are God's specialty. So keep pressing, keep trying, and keep believing. You have to get it into your beautiful mind first and tell

Listen, comebacks are God's specialty.

---

[18]https://hbr.org/2017/02/women-are-less-likely-to-apply-for-executive-roles-if-theyve-been-rejected-before

yourself until you are convinced that regardless of the turns in your journey indeed *You are Worthy!*

Properly sitting in the position of your worth is also connected to the revelation of God's presence and power that is within us. It's a challenging point to contend with, but we can deeply love Jesus, know him to be real and a real part of our lives, but still struggle to make the connection that it is indeed His selfsame power that is resident and available within us daily! If you are a believer in Christ Jesus, you are a new creature in Him.[19] His precious Holy Spirit lives within those who believe![20] We truly have a superpower! In fact, it is part of our role as the redeemed of Christ to actively live that shine and bring witness to others of the glory of the Lord that is the head of our lives.[21] I am sure you have experienced people whose talent belies their success or whose position is far exceeded by their skill, but who are not at all short on confidence and belief in themselves, what they can do, and where they belong. On the other hand, when it comes to us as children of God, the adversarial mission is great to keep our minds trapped by small thinking and distracted from the revelation of our temple existence- that we house the divine power and spirit of the Holy Ghost within.[22] When you are equally vigilant to rest your thoughts on that fact daily, and your position as the temple of the Holy Ghost, your

---

[19] 2 Corinthians 5:17
[20] Romans 8:9
[21] Matthew 5:16
[22] 1 Corinthians 6:19-19

perspective of your worthiness for the call will certainly shift from one that is self-focused to a perspective focused on the one who has called you.

CHAPTER 9

Key Mindset Strategy #3
Legacy Focused

We should always have three friends in our lives.
One who walks ahead who we look up to and follow,
One who walks beside us who is with us every step of our journey
One we reach back for and bring along after we've cleared the way.

-MICHELLE OBAMA

I am so grateful that you decided to take this journey with me. I am so blessed that God directed you to these pages and connected our paths in this way. I find it so fitting that we land here as our concluding chapter at Chapter 9, the number of birth and new beginnings. I pray that you will live with all splendor and joy the new beginnings of a purposeful, fulfilling and empowered re-imagined lifestyle. You learned insights to uncover and give birth to life-changing vision, take your queues to evaluate that vision as you evolve, and re-imagine your life for next level purposes in your journey. You are well on your way to living the Re-Imagined lifestyle. And as you do, there is one final key to this picture that must fill our motivations and should impact our mindsets towards our direction, and that is to be legacy focused women.

This journey, and your victory in it, is much bigger than just you. It is about those who are silently looking and inspired by you, those for whom you are clearing a way, and those who are coming long after.

Keeping the motivation of leaving a solid legacy as your gift expands the way you do business and the way you dream. It will stretch what you see in your re-imagination process. And being legacy focused will motivate you beyond your comfort level to manifest the most impactful ends for the sake of a larger purpose.

Being legacy focused speaks to your generosity, your commitment to having a lasting impact on this world and in the lives of others and your enduring commitment to the Kingdom. It's much like caring for the environment and recycling. You have a choice, but doing so has gains, the greatest of which may not even be felt in your lifetime. And so it is the same in principle as we consider what is the message we will leave as our legacy when we re-imagine and up-level vision along the way.

Legacy expands your perspective and impact

When we are mindful to care about how our service and our journey will enrich other's lives in lasting ways, that generosity expands our perspective and up-levels the weight of our impact and even the weight of the opportunities that flow towards us in our re-imagined seasons.

I couldn't be more grateful for utilizing the inspirations God has revealed throughout this book to re-imagine my own life. To coach women and women leaders of faith and support their success, speak and inspire groups in a range of platforms and make room to diligently support the visions of my precious family is rich beyond measure. I've even enjoyed representing global brands such as Disney, Panera Bread and others in the commercial and talent space by pulling up those little Keitra imaginations and putting some warrior princess action and faith towards them.

But another vision piece I have seen for some time for me and my husband was helping others grow as entrepreneurs and become empowered financially and in ownership. The how and the fine print continue to be uncovered along the way, but it is part of the vision I have seen all the same. But, if I had not shifted to be legacy minded, I am sure I would have missed how God was opening a door that aligns with that vision. In fact, what is funny for me to consider now is that whenever a contact would approach me with a "business opportunity," I would go (well sometimes run) in the other direction.

Fortunately, I was at a place in which I had grown hungry for legacy and legacy building principles so I allowed myself to at least be a bit more curious. I'm glad that I did because I realized that what was being shared with me was less of the type of opportunity that came to my mind and more of an opportunity for me to learn. I didn't have to build a team or sell a product (which I certainly support by the way), but a bit more aligned with what gets me fired up was an opportunity to learn- to learn a skill towards wealth building and the application of investment strategies that I interestingly had already been seeking. Had I not had the right mindset, I would have dismissed an opportunity that aligns with my passions, helps me learn market and investment strategies that I can pass on to my loved ones, and provides a learning and business building community that I can share with others. This is vision! Now, I take great joy in co-learning with my kids as I continue to learn, build, and get supported by community as an investor and solid market trader. It's empowering as a woman leader! But I certainly would have missed a purposeful alignment to have significant and lasting impact in the lives of my children, family, and others but for being pre-occupied with a view towards legacy personally and in the in the way of service to others.

We are undoubtedly able to more generously help and serve our homes, communities, and others when we are awake to our financial legacy as one legacy focus. But the idea is for you to explore the picture of legacy for yourself as far more expansive than your financial legacy alone. So take a moment and consider, what might a lasting legacy look like for you?

When we are legacy focused with deep care and stewardship of the lasting impact we will have on the lives of others through our life's message and the things we set our hands to do, God will provide generous opportunities to meet your generous mindset. Generosity begets generosity. And the legacy mindset is a generous mindset.

You may recall my big blown up prayer I placed on the room wall while I was hospitalized with baby Legend. The idea was to consistently draw my focus towards that declaration daily but also to help edify the hearts and hopes of the medical team each time they visited. They were highly invested in our care. My intention had both a personal and community focus. One day, before I was released from the hospital, the nursing team approached me and asked if they could leave that prayer up permanently on the wall to encourage and support the faith of the next mothers who would have to use that room in the future. I tear up even as I write as it is powerful to think of our story, our faith, our journey, and God's victory in it continuing to encourage mothers and families long after we were gone who were experiencing crisis in extenuating ways as did we. Generous legacy producing opportunity will find you when you are first generous in your intent.

Being legacy focused as a matter of our re-imagined discipline widens the breadth of our visions and even opens the door for opportunity to generously return to us in abounding measure.

~

Closing thoughts

As we bring to a close this part of our re-imagined journey, it really all now begins. I hope this journey has opened up tremendous inspiration towards the best days of your life. What a truly blessed time in sharing with you each and every word you found here my friend. I pray you have been blessed, met, and enriched by your reading.

I pray that the wind of God's divine inspiration is constantly at your back. That your ability to see, hear and be directed by the almighty presence of God is heightened and released in great measure. I pray for clarity like never before and a discipline empowered by God's grace and anointing. I pray for the courage to dream big dreams, the wisdom to keep God in them, and the ability to embrace transition and evolution with strength and strategy that gives birth to next level purposes, maturity, and insight. I pray for strength in your mind, peace in your heart and healing in your body that you can run your race without hindrance and with strength. Blessings I pray to you dear sister in every way today and always.

In Jesus precious name I pray.

Amen

The guide ahead is a significant part of this journey and will help further shape your experience in being a woman of vision and establishing a visionary lifestyle.

PART 3

360 VISION
SELF-COACHING GUIDE

Gift yourself the time,
a peaceful environment
and focus for these reflections.

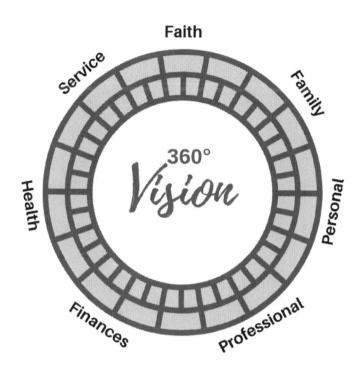

THE 360 VISION

*There is no passion to be found playing small - in settling
for a life that is less than the one you are capable of living.*

NELSON MANDELA

We have walked through the significant way that vision is designed as a divinely inspired, sustaining and motivating guide to our lives. It's a far richer concept than might ordinarily be afforded it. When vision is utilized with intention in our lives, shifts in alignment, victory and even our overall sense of happiness can be the welcomed result. We also see, as in the life and experience of King Jehoshaphat and the people of Judah, that God inspired vision stretches beyond mediocrity and presses the boundaries of extraordinary. So ladies, as we continue our journeys in life as empowered women who develop and operate with complete vision in the 360 areas of our lives (faith, family, personal, professional, finance, health, and service), we must hold captive the thoughts and truths about ourselves that:

We are indeed fearfully and wonderfully made, strong to bear the weight of great, extraordinary in our design, exquisite in the complexity of our minds, brilliant in our creative sense, elegant in our design and gifts, built to withstand challenge and trouble and graced with the wisdom to nurture greatness within us and in others. We are extraordinary![23]

You, my friend, are an extraordinary being, created by an extraordinary Father so before we do the work of building 360 vision around our lives, you must get it right in your mind now that it is absolutely OK and consistent with our extraordinary Creator to believe in visions requiring extraordinary belief.

Ok, so now that we have that important business settled, in moving through the components of a complete vision and the 360 vision that taps into the whole picture of our lives, let's begin with the component of faith. *(By the way, this is a perfect place to utilize the journal I have provided for you in the adjacent section.)* Your vision for faith speaks to your faith walk and what you most desire that to look like for you. It is easy to see vision as a no-brainer in certain areas of our lives such as our careers for instance, but our vision should be very clear and considered regarding how we express ourselves genuinely and

---

[23] Extraordinary Woman: The Affirmation, Keitra Robinson, J.D.

uniquely through our faith. Otherwise, we can create another subtle opportunity to walk in insufficiency and longing because of a lack of vision. For as we know, without a vision the people, what?... "they perish." You got it!

If you are expectant and put your heart, mind, and intention towards it, I am confident that you will enjoy how the Holy Spirit collaborates with you and helps you see more of yourself and more clearly where you want to be. I pray revelation, inspiration, and clarification as you walk through these first steps of vision casting in your 360 areas of focus.

-FAITH VISION PROMPTS-

With those intentions in mind, wholeheartedly consider the picture of yourself in the area of your faith that is sincere and heartfelt for you. It may even be that you have never articulated to anyone certain things you have seen or imagined for yourself in the way of your faith and your spiritual journey. Sometimes that is because of the courage needed to receive the big bold visions that God is looking for us to embrace. This is a wonderful time to honestly capture those thoughts.

Now, these prompts are not all-inclusive. I encourage you to expect the Holy Spirit to help bring additional questions and thoughts to you as you actively consider and journal during your time of reflection. You should prayerfully explore that vision that has roots in your heart, is satisfying, ideal, gives room for God's power and grace to be active in the fruition of that vision, is joyful and is complete. Expect that this will be an empowering time for you as you give time for God to inspire your imagination and thoughts towards your vision in each area of 360 focus.

1. How satisfied are you with your spiritual life and faith walk on a scale from 1-10 (10 being the most satisfied)?

   If not a 9-10, what would need to change to get you there?

2. What is a picture of yourself as it relates to your spiritual maturation and faith that you believe deep down most represents what you are to look like even if you feel you are far from it right now?

3. Imagine for a bit.

   Close your eyes and imagine yourself and the faith component of your life being at a 9 or 10? Now write down every word that describes that picture and immediately comes to mind.

   They do not need to be connected, just the first honest, pure words that come up for you when you make that visualization.

   Consider that picture holistically from your church community, friends in fellowship, knowledge, and understanding of the Bible, understanding of your spiritual gifts, calling, family and faith, your service to your faith community, how your faith aligns in your daily work....

4. What frustrates you about the current status of your faith and spiritual journey?

5. What is in need of change and is within your control to change?

6. What does the prayer life look like for the woman you most desire to see in yourself?

7. How are you growing in your knowledge and understanding of scripture?

8. How diligent and consistent are you with pursuing biblical and spiritual knowledge? How diligent and consistent do you want to be?

9. How are you serving in your faith?

10. What do you want your service to the church and your church community to look like?

11. What sense of calling might you feel?

    Is your current commitment and path consistent with that?

12. How fresh and consistent are your spiritual revelations?

13. Are you as mature in your faith as you desire? If not, what are some steps you can take to advance your growth.

14. What does your faith community and fellowship look like?

    What do you want it to most look like?

15. If someone close to you were to share their experience with you and your faith, what would they say?

    What would you want them to say?

16. What conflicts if any do you experience with your faith values and your career or work experiences, if any?

17. How does your current work support or align with your faith values?

18. How satisfied are you with your faith walk and what do you need to shift, if anything, to be inspired and satisfied by it?

19. What is holding you back from your spiritual growth?

20. What hurts or experiences may be affecting your relationship with your faith and community of faith?

    What steps might you take towards healing and resolution?

21. Who do you admire in your faith and why do you admire them? How can their example help inspire your vision for yourself?

22. How much have you considered your part and significance in the work of the Kingdom of God?

23. How are you intentionally committing to shining the light of Christ in your various fields of influence either strategically or directly?

    Wrap up: Take a moment to review all of your inspired thoughts and reflections. Begin to put the picture together of what your heart is showing you that you most desire for yourself in relationship to your faith now that you have taken the time to reflect and imagine with the limits off.

From that picture begin to formulate and record affirmations in the form of "I am" statements. Who is that woman that you see?

~FAMILY/RELATIONSHIPS VISION PROMPTS~

Your vision for your family and relationships relates to the envisioned future you most desire for yourself in relationship to your household, extended family and close relationships. This is an area for which I want to encourage you to be sure to contemplatively rest and reflect. Relationship, and God's intention through it, is so powerful and foundational even to our creation and God's original plan.

For God so loved the world that he gave his only begotten son[24]…

It is through relationship that we can see the purest expression of Christ, His love and how we should endeavor to express that love. We grow in our understanding of Christ and his love through relationship. Intention and vision towards this 360 area of vision carries rich dividends. A Harvard Review study, in fact, one of the world's longest studies of adult life, concluded that close relationships more than

---

[24] John 3:16 KJV

money or fame are what keep people happy throughout their lives.[25] So let's invest our time here as we walk our empowered journey to a place of fulfillment. Let God inspire your reflections and expect Him to guide you to additional and specific vision prompts for your life.

~

Single:

1. What is your heart's desire and vision for your immediate (nuclear) family? What is that picture? Who is in that picture?

    a. Once you have that picture in mind, zoom in on yourself. Describe the woman that you see. What is her presence? What are her strengths? What has she overcome? What has she accomplished? What are her emotions? What are her strengths in a relationship? What do her immediate family members say about her? How much time does she spend with her family? How does she spend that time? What are her most valued contributions?

    b. What shifts if any, which are within your control, can you make to align with that vision of yourself?

2. How can you absolutely maximize your single season?

---

[25]https://news.harvard.edu/gazette/story/2017/04/over-nearly-80-years-harvard-study-has-been-showing-how-to-live-a-healthy-and-happy-life/

What inspired pursuits or areas of focus, both significant and perhaps less dynamic (but equally important), might God be making room for you to lend your attention to in this season? Consider all areas of your life that come up for you.

3. How committed are you to invest in close relationships/ friendships in this season?

Married:

4. When you think of your home life, what emotions immediately come to mind?

   Now imagine your home life and immediate family representing all that you would dream it to be. What emotions come up for you?

   How are those emotions different or the same? What shifts within your control and consistent with your faith values can you make to align yourself with your imagined home life where needed?

5. What experiences do you dream of sharing with your spouse?

6. What areas in your family life and vision need to evolve as you have evolved over the years?

7. What do you know about your husband's vision for himself? How aware are you of his goals and desires? How are you able to support his vision?

8. How much of yourself and time are you investing with intention in your marriage and home life? Is your current investment where it needs to be? What do you desire it to look like?

9. If you have children, what is your vision for each of your children? Consider things such as:

    How do you want them to show up in the world?

    What do you want their spiritual lives to look like?

    What areas of exposure and experience do you want them to have?

    What does their education and learning experiences look like? How are they educated?

    How do you wish for your children to relate to you?

    How do you wish for your children to relate to others and the world?

    What memories do you wish for them to have of you?

    What words do you want your children to use to describe you? What are the words you would use to describe your children?

    What experiences do you dream of sharing with your children?

    How aligned are you with achieving those reflections at present. What do you need to shift, if anything to get there?

General:

10. What do you think your family (both nuclear and extended) would say if they described your commitment to them?

    Would the response likely reflect what you would most want them to say? If not, how so? What shifts if any might you be prompted to consider?

11. Close your eyes for a moment and imagine that you are happy, content and nearly overwhelmed with joy about your family life both nuclear and extended.

    What do you see in that picture?

    Who do you see in that picture?

    What shifts that are within your control and which are consistent with your faith values might you make to align with that envisioned future?

12. What can you do to increase the level of contentment in relationships with family members both nuclear and extended that are presently frustrating or lacking?

    What things are within your control?

    What things are not within my control?

    How well are you resting in trust with God about those things outside of your control?

13. How committed are you to cultivating close friendships?

14. What do you envision your desired and ideal friendship circle to look like?

15. How and how often do you spend time with your close friends?

16. What relationships within your family need more of your attention?

17. What areas in your family life and relationships now need to evolve as you have evolved over the years? In what ways?

18. What is the picture like of your relationship with your extended family that you most desire?

    Wrap up: Take a moment to review all of your inspired thoughts and reflections. Begin to put the picture together of what your heart is showing you that you most desire for yourself in relationship to your family/relationships now that you have taken the time to reflect and imagine with the limits off.

    From that picture begin to formulate and record affirmations in the form of "I am" statements. Who is that woman that you see?

~PERSONAL VISION PROMPTS~

Your personal vision relates to the mark you will leave on this world. What will be your legacy, the footprints you leave, the way that you are remembered and the message you telegraph through your life? Your personal vision wakes you up! It snaps you out of neutral because you are aware of the significant role you play in a greater Kingdom purpose. Your personal vision should inspire you, excite you, motivate you, and definitely challenge you.

1. What legacy do you want to leave and who are the people (and groups) your legacy will most affect?

2. If money were not an issue, what would you do with your life to have the most impact and capture ideas about which you have long dreamt?

3. When you were a young girl, what were some of your dreams for yourself? How often do those dreams come up for you now? How aligned is your life currently with any of those dreams? If you

could, would you recapture any of those dreams for your life today that you haven't already?

4. If God were speaking in plain audible language to you right now, looking you square in the face and were desperately nudging and encouraging you to just go for it! "I've got you!" What would those things be God is referencing?

5. Imagine you fully embraced your opportunity to conquer your fears and empty yourself of your gifts and dreams during your lifetime, what are the things for which you will be remembered?

6. What are the descriptive words you wish people who remember your life would use when thinking of you?

7. How consistent are your personal dreams with an omnipotent God?

    What shifts, if any, are you inspired to make in how you view what is possible in your life and what is possible through your life?

8. What are the values you would say you presently project through your life? (for instance, excellence, charity, etc.)

    What are the values you most desire to project through your life?

9. What would you say are your best attributes? How consistent are you with exemplifying those attributes?

    Wrap up: Take a moment to review all of your inspired thoughts and reflections. Begin to put the picture together of what your heart is showing you that you most desire for yourself in relationship to your personal vision now that you have taken the time to reflect and imagine with the limits off.

From that picture begin to formulate and record affirmations in the form of "I am" statements. Who is that woman that you see?

~PROFESSIONAL VISION PROMPTS~

Your vision for your profession captures the ways in which you put your hands to work to offer your gifts, skills, and talents to the world.

Women are uniquely equipped to nurture in a nuanced and intuitive way to include nurturing vision. For instance, mothers can hear a cry and just "know" the baby needs food, or needs a diaper change or simply needs their attention. Similarly, as we nurture the ideas and visions of others in the marketplace, we too must honor our intuitive sense to "know" not only what the needs are for other's visions to which we are assigned, but stay very connected to hearing our own voice and nurturing those needs and shifts that are crying out to us in the midst of that bigger picture. It's a unique dance all our own as women, but we are brilliantly equipped for it. We must nurture in that unique intuitive way both within and outside of ourselves.

For instance, we may nurture the ideas and vision of our company's leadership, but we still need not lose sight of nurturing the ideas and vision we have for our own professional vision. There are times we may find the two simply can no longer co-exist-that our professional visions have outgrown where we are. Nurturing is nuanced, and it is natural. That is one reason I wanted to rest here for a bit because it is easy for us to get lost in nurturing others and lose sight of maximizing the gifts we are to offer the world ourselves. We can get stuck and lose sight of ourselves if we don't give time to our own professional visions and are mindful to richly nurture them as well.

So with that in mind, I want to encourage you to vision cast and reflect on your profession in seasons. Although your professional vision may not shift dramatically, considering your vision in seasons is important because perhaps your professional vision may shift a bit or a lot as you grow a family, or grow a business. Perhaps you desire a shift as your children move into adulthood or as you approach the time that many would call "retirement." (By the way, I personally don't encourage that word. Our words have active energy that they produce. In fact, many have literally and unfortunately "retired" in body because they have been telling themselves and directing their energy towards retirement for so long! So instead, it's simply time to shift!)

Your profession is how you offer your gifts, skills and talents to the world and everybody's paths are as unique as those gifts, talents and the diversity of expressions in which they are offered to others. But setting vision towards your profession is the way in which we maximize our unique impact and make sure life isn't just happening to us but that we are making life happen!

~

1. What seasons of life might you naturally define for yourself? You might consider 3-4 seasons that you might see for your life.

   [By way of example: first half of career, second half of career, golden years]

2. Consider each of those seasons, what will you look like when you are maximizing the unique skills, gifts, and design God has given you to share abundantly for His glory?

3. In what ways has God uniquely designed you to significantly impact the lives of others?

4. What are the talents and skills that you bring to the table that are uniquely your own? In what ways are you or can you maximize those gift in the marketplace?

   Coaching tip: I do want to take a moment and empower you a bit as you reflect on your unique talents and skills because sometimes it is hardest for us to define our own. We can sometimes miss our gifts because they have been shrouded in overuse. For instance, let's say you have constantly been told that you talk too much or that you talk too harshly. Well, the good news is, you would likely have a gift hidden under that overuse such as your ability to see past fluff, your strength at being bold enough to be a straight shooter, the ability to easily connect with people, or your deep curiosity. So take your time here as you explore. And don't be afraid to ask someone close to you for their thoughts regarding your unique gifts as well.

5.   If money and resources were not an issue, what type of work would you do in the different stages of life you have defined for yourself?

(Work here is not limited to a job but the work of your attention and hands meaning the activity and commitment during each season to utilizing and offering your gifts and talents to others.)

6.   What did you dream of doing with your life as a child?

What was exciting about that dream?

List those things that attracted you to those dreams? What things are you duplicating in your life now from those childhood dreams or the things that may have attracted you to those dreams?

If your response is limited, on a scale from 1-10 (with 10 being the "most desired"), how much do you currently desire to tap into more of those childhood longings?

7.   What are some of your unique personality traits?

8. On a scale of 1-10 (10 being the most), how intentional have you been in navigating the course of your work?

9. Where do you want to be in your life's work 10 years from now? What is that picture? How are you on course to align with that picture of yourself? What do you need to do to prepare?

10. How is your life's work impacting others?

11. In what ways could your professional life be more satisfying and fulfilling?

12. What has kept you from making moves to shift into a more satisfying place?

Wrap up: Take a moment to review all of your inspired thoughts and reflections. Begin to put the picture together of what your heart is showing you that you most desire for yourself in relationship to your professional vision now that you have taken the time to reflect and imagine with the limits off.

From that picture begin to formulate and record affirmations in the form of "I am" statements. Who is that woman that you see?

~FINANCIAL VISION PROMPTS~

Vision in the area of our finances is critical because it shifts our mental and spiritual consciousness and conversations to those that are spoken over us from heaven. We must be ever aware that there is a diabolical strategy in consistent and oppressive financial distress for the people of God. So then we must be equally strategic and focused towards our financial empowerment. Your vision here, as in all areas of your 360 vision, is about strategy and empowerment.

Our spiritual inheritance is liberty. So we must take the time to create a vision that is filled with the freedom that God's grace has afforded us as his beloved so we can begin to shift or shift even more. A financial vision will up-level our belief system, wake us up to what is possible, shift our actions and decisions and motivate us to operate with a Kingdom mindset and authority.

Some of you ladies may already have taken the time, energy and reflection towards this area and have formulated a financial vision for yourselves that has affected your belief and behavior and of which you experience the fruit of daily. But for most women reading, I know this to be an area in which we must take the time to focus as statistics consistently show us that the majority of people find their greatest source of stress to be financially related. Financial distress significantly affects health, marriages, and even the health of our children who feel the strain.[26] Taking your time here as you reflect will help you begin to see the picture of yourself you wish to see financially and that you believe heaven has written for you. More importantly, you will set the stage for your motivations and actions to begin to be directed and constrained by that inspired picture for yourself and family. Setting financial vision helps position us to move in a proactive way rather than getting stuck in a cyclical pattern that keeps us from giving and serving at our best levels.

1. What does financial freedom mean to you?

2. Describe what financial freedom would look like for you.

3. What scriptures influence your thoughts around money?

4. How do you believe God wants you to live financially? What are some guiding scriptures for that belief?

5. What type of financial legacy do you want to leave and to whom? Be specific about what you would like that to look like.

---

[26] http://www.apa.org/monitor/2015/04/money-stress.aspx

6. What significant experiences do you want for yourself (and your family)?

7. Where are some places you dream to travel? Who would travel with you?

8. What organizations, charities, people and/or services do you want to be free to support financially? How much do you want to be able to give to them?

9. What do you ultimately want your financial investments to look like? In what ways do you want to invest or expand your investments?

10. What were some of the messages you heard growing up that could be limiting your beliefs around money, if any? What statements or pictures of yourself would you use to replace those limiting beliefs?

11. Name a person or persons with a financial legacy that you strongly admire. What are some of the reasons that you admire them in that way?

12. When you think of a prosperous person, how would you describe them?

13. When you think of a greedy person, how would you describe them?

14. How clear are you with the difference between prosperity and greed for yourself?

15. What do you want your financial literacy to look like?

16. How consistent is your network of relationships and mentors with the type of person you are working towards in your financial vision of yourself?

17. What types of training, events, networks, and associations do you envision yourself utilizing to become even more financially empowered and strong?

18. What are your strengths around your finances?

19. Paint a picture of yourself in the area of your finances as you would most desire your financial picture to look 5, 10, even 20 years from now? Describe those pictures.

    In what areas do you need to grow financially in understanding, experience, and exposure to achieve that picture?

    What actions could you take to support your growth in those areas?

20. List all of your financial dreams.

    Wrap up: Take a moment to review all of your inspired thoughts and reflections. Begin to put the picture together of what your heart is showing you that you most desire for yourself in relationship to your financial vision now that you have taken the time to reflect and imagine with the limits off.

From that picture begin to formulate and record affirmations in the form of "I am" statements. Who is that woman that you see?

~HEALTH VISION PROMPTS~

Our health vision relates to how we envision ourselves when we maximize our health potential and exemplify our commitment to honor God's gift to us through our bodies. I have become quite convinced over time that very often the more we grow in our revelations of God and the God within us the more we naturally desire to be more disciplined and "temple" focused. But even so, it doesn't mean we can win on auto-pilot in this area. As always, we need a strategy. And vision is part of that strategy towards our motivation, consistency, and belief. As well, our commitment to our health can be an underrated but significant piece of the puzzle to our overall sense of well-being, happiness and fulfillment.

Our health and well-being will not only shift the trajectory of our productivity from a practical level, but from a spiritual perspective, it helps us operate with a sense of alignment and gratification knowing that we have bridled our actions to honor the gift of our bodies God has offered us. As women of faith, walking in our disciplined health is powerful, inspiring, redeeming, wise, authoritative, gratifying, life producing, life extending, spiritual and rewarding.

Ultimately, being intentional and disciplined towards our health and fitness is about stewardship. Let's look at it this way. Just as we wouldn't go into a church or place of worship, consistently fill it and leave it a mess with junk, never maintaining the interior or exterior grounds, letting things that are broken remain unfixed without attention for years, and allowing it to get so run down and so out of shape that the building can not be used for God's glory as intended or to the extent it was intended, so too it is with us. We can't ignore caring deeply for our body's and as believers not fairly accept the inconsistency in that, albeit a difficult pill to swallow at times. Our health vision and keeping to that vision is an opportunity to nurture our fulfillment rather than empower our frustration.

Do you not know that your bodies are temples of the Holy Spirit, who is in you, whom you have received from God? You are not your own;[27]

Honoring our temples increases our energy, strengthens our focus, advances our endurance, benefits our emotional well-being, and allows us to serve our purposes more freely and unencumbered. Our health and our part in it, how we prioritize our health, our spiritual

---

[27] 1 Corinthians 6:19 NIV

perspective on our health discipline and our revelation of our health as part of our success plan is all massive to our big picture.

~

1. Imagine you are a strong representation of radiance, health, well-being, fitness, happiness, mental clarity, and energy. Create that picture of yourself in your mind.

    Who are the people who are most affected or influenced by the "you" that you see? How are they affected or influenced by you?

2. When you consider the word "health-prosperity" how would you define that word for yourself?

3. How would your life change if you were living fully in a zone of health-prosperity and taking control of those things related to your health and well-being that are within your control?

4. What things about your current lifestyle reflect your commitment to your health?

5. What things about your current lifestyle need to change to reflect your desires towards optimal health?

6. Imagine yourself at your optimal level of health and living in a zone that you most aspire for yourself? Describe everything about that lady you can think of from her emotions, activities, how she engages with others, her social life… every detail that comes to mind.

What shifts for good do you identify in that picture of yourself?

7. How empowered are you about nutrition and healthy living? Does that knowledge align with that vision of yourself that you explored at your optimal health? What new steps or shifts do you identify you should take to become more knowledgeable about your health and nutrition, if any?

8. What areas of healthy living are you most naturally motivated?

9. What areas of healthy living do you need the most support? How have you sought that support or how might you as part of your lifestyle?

10. Who are people within your close network that inspire you with regards to health and well-being?

11. What scriptures are the most profound in motivating you towards living strong in your health? (Feel free to research)

Wrap up: Take a moment to review all of your inspired thoughts and reflections. Begin to put the picture together of what your heart is showing you that you most desire for yourself in relationship to your health vision now that you have taken the time to reflect and imagine with the limits off.

From that picture begin to formulate and record affirmations in the form of "I am" statements. Who is that woman that you see?

~SERVICE VISION PROMPTS~

There is something that I have taught for years, and this is that purpose is plural. Our purposes are connected to and are in relationship to others. If utilizing our gifts in a meaningful way and doing so in connection with others is not a part of our purpose plan, we aren't quite aligned just yet. Scripture is consistent with models and patterns of purpose that are relationship driven. For instance, we were created to multiply God's light and presence on this earth. We are a connected body to complete His purposes. Woman was created for collaborative partnership with man. Jesus's entire life was to guide a lost world by His example in life and save a lost world through His death. So then our connection and care towards others is a significant way in which we are designed to function fully and at our best.

It is well documented that serving others has significant benefits on our health, happiness and life satisfaction. But I must say. I don't find that at all surprising. It is that we are simply aligning ourselves with our natural and intended design.[28] Our purpose is plural, not a

---

[28] https://www.ncbi.nlm.nih.gov/pmc/articles/PMC5504679/

singular focused journey. So with that, serving others is likely already a natural draw and connection for you. But in setting our visions for service, we want to explore how can we not only bring this area of vision more completely into view but maximize how we offer ourselves to others in our lifetime.

❧

1. Ask God to help you see some of the most courageous ways that He might have you offer your gifts, talents, time and resources to others? Also, consider some visions that may have long been coming up for you but for which you might not yet have acted on.

    What are some of the ideas that come to mind?

2. If you were to integrate serving others as a significant theme in your life, what might that look like for you?

3. What are some of your current limitations in serving as richly as your heart might desire? In what ways that are within your control might you begin to orchestrate shifts to make room for those desires?

4. Have you mentally formulated seasons in your life that you see yourself more abundantly in serving others? When are those seasons? How would you maximize your time now to set up those visions?

5. What, if any, projects, ideas, or missions have you often thought of and perhaps never acted on or shared because they seemed too big?

6. What, if any, projects, ideas, or missions have you often thought of and perhaps never acted on or shared because they seemed out of time?

7. In what ways can you shift your mindset in certain commitments to be more mindful of opportunities to serve and volunteer your gifts and talents for the benefit of others?

8. What legacy do you want to leave in the way of charity and service?

9. What are the ways in which you can integrate volunteering and serving more seamlessly into your life?

10. How committed are you to mentoring others? How would you like that level of commitment to change, if at all?

11. What groups could benefit from your wisdom, gifts, skills, time and interest?

12. If time were not an issue how would you increase your footprint in the way of volunteerism? What organizations, issues, missions tug at your heart?

13. Consider the people you most influence. How will they be affected by the example of your diligent commitment to others?

14. How can you incorporate others with whom you have influence in your service vision and double your impact by also serving them by your mentorship?

Wrap up: Take a moment to review all of your inspired thoughts and reflections. Begin to put the picture together of what your heart is showing you that you most desire for yourself in relationship to your vision for service now that you have taken the time to reflect and imagine with the limits off.

From that picture begin to formulate and record affirmations in the form of "I am" statements. Who is that woman that you see?

PUTTING IT ALL TOGETHER

Then the LORD replied: "Write down the revelation and make it plain on tablets so that a herald may run with it."

HABAKKUK 2:2

Write the vision:

Vision Statements- Now that you have begun to stir up the visions in your heart, you can put together guiding statements that plainly communicate the vision that you see for yourself in your seven areas of 360 vision. Here you would formulate about 5-6 statements for each area.

This is a good time to make sure that you have included all of the ingredients to your re-imagined life recipe: (1) that you have considered how you have evolved over time, (2) you have considered places that need an upgrade, (2) you have considered what "little you" dreamt and is still whispering to you today.

<u>Making it Plain:</u>

Vision Boards- Vision Boarding is a fun and highly effective way to bring life to your vision and draw your faith and actions in the direction of your vision. There are many ways to do vision boards from digital displays, poster boards, shadow boxes and the like. Because I like the references on my board to be rather exact, I personally enjoy creating a digital poster collage by pulling images from online and my personal stash and then uploading them to a local photo store to create a poster-sized collage. They frame well, are large and are easy to duplicate.

But there is no one specific way to vision board, just make it meaningful and enjoyable! In fact, some people really enjoy the treasure hunt of working through magazines to pull reference pictures and words to create boards. That is often the most utilized way when I do workshops, and it's a lot of fun especially if you want to grab a few friends and go at it together.

Although there is no specific way to create a board, there are however some important tips and principles you should keep in mind to make it most effective.

Be sure to use words and insert them among the visual pieces you add to your board. Research indicates that adding "action words" to your vision board makes an important psychological connection for you and increases the effectiveness of your vision board by telling your mind what you need to do to accomplish what is to that you see.

For example: exercise, network, juice veggies, study craft, pray

Make sure to keep your vision board in a prominent place. It is important to daily visualize and see your vision board, in the same way, saying your affirmations are important daily. Your vision board is effective not because of some mystical reason but because it is a reflection of not only the science of psychology but Biblical direction. When you make the vision plain, you are giving your action, intentions, thoughts, and faith a law to follow. When you constantly see and tell yourself to eat healthy, eventually your actions naturally line up with what you see. As we discussed in our section on mental fortitude in part 2, you are feeding the *loins of your mind* the language and pictures to reproduce for you consistently rather than less productive or purposeful thoughts and ideas.

If you create your board in a format in which it can be duplicated, place a copy in various prominent places. For instance, I have one directly eye shot across from me when I wake up, I have a small picture on my bathroom mirror, and I have one placed in a beautiful frame on my desk. Yes, I am overload! But there is nothing like retiring a vision board because everything you have placed on it has manifested and I have indeed had that joyous experience. Ah-ma-zing!

3. Make the process special. The vision boarding process should be special and something you look forward to doing. Include friends or build corporate boards with your teams. Engage just the right music, include some of your favorite snacks, and have a good time. Teach your children to vision board and even do it as a family. Our kids love dreaming and collaborating together for family dreams. Make this a success strategy for the entire family, and something you all look forward to doing. It's a big deal because you are revealing to the world and the atmosphere the big bold destination to which you will without doubt arrive.

Let your visions be your law

*Where there is no vision, the people are unrestrained, but happy is he who **keeps the law**.*
PROVERBS 29:18 NASB

Finally know that your power comes in your commitment to daily keep before you and follow your visions like they are the law governing your daily actions, beliefs, and motivations. Like "Flo Jo," return to the pages of your journal until it literally falls apart from use! Feed your mind and feed your atmosphere with champion-like discipline and commitment by daily repeating your affirmations, reading your vision statements and seeing your visions expressed visually throughout your day through your vision boards or visual prompts.

Record yourself repeating your affirmations and vision statements and play them daily as travel to work, exercise or as part of your time of devotion. Post your affirmations on your shower door or bathroom mirror and speak them daily. Do *all* you can do to be deeply committed to the power of vision being an active, daily, presence and discipline in your life.

Life Re-Imagined Journal

_____

_____

_____

_____

_____

_____

_____

_____

_____

_____

_____

_____

_____

_____

_____

_____

_____

_____

_____

_____

_____

_____

_____

_____

Life Re-Imagined Journal

Life Re-Imagined Journal

_____

_____

_____

_____

_____

_____

_____

_____

_____

_____

_____

_____

_____

_____

_____

_____

_____

_____

_____

_____

_____

_____

Life Re-Imagined Journal

Life Re-Imagined Journal

_____

_____

_____

_____

_____

_____

_____

_____

_____

_____

_____

_____

_____

_____

_____

_____

_____

_____

_____

_____

_____

_____

_____

_____

Life Re-Imagined Journal

_____

_____

_____

_____

_____

_____

_____

_____

_____

_____

_____

_____

_____

_____

_____

_____

_____

_____

_____

_____

_____

_____

Life Re-Imagined Journal

_____

_____

_____

_____

_____

_____

_____

_____

_____

_____

_____

_____

_____

_____

_____

_____

_____

_____

_____

_____

_____

_____

Life Re-Imagined Journal

Life Re-Imagined Journal

_____

_____

_____

_____

_____

_____

_____

_____

_____

_____

_____

_____

_____

_____

_____

_____

_____

_____

_____

_____

_____

_____

_____

_____

_____

_____

_____

Life Re-Imagined Journal

Life Re-Imagined Journal

_____

_____

_____

_____

_____

_____

_____

_____

_____

_____

_____

_____

_____

_____

_____

_____

_____

_____

_____

_____

_____

_____

_____

_____

Life Re-Imagined Journal

Life Re-Imagined Journal

Life Re-Imagined Journal

_____

_____

_____

_____

_____

_____

_____

_____

_____

_____

_____

_____

_____

_____

_____

_____

_____

_____

_____

_____

_____

_____

Life Re-Imagined Journal

Life Re-Imagined Journal

_____

_____

_____

_____

_____

_____

_____

_____

_____

_____

_____

_____

_____

_____

_____

_____

_____

_____

_____

_____

_____

_____

_____

Life Re-Imagined Journal

_____
_____
_____
_____
_____
_____
_____
_____
_____
_____
_____
_____
_____
_____
_____
_____
_____
_____
_____
_____
_____
_____
_____

Life Re-Imagined Journal

_____

_____

_____

_____

_____

_____

_____

_____

_____

_____

_____

_____

_____

_____

_____

_____

_____

_____

_____

_____

_____

_____

_____

_____

Life Re-Imagined Journal

Life Re-Imagined Journal

_____

_____

_____

_____

_____

_____

_____

_____

_____

_____

_____

_____

_____

_____

_____

_____

_____

_____

_____

_____

_____

_____

_____

_____

_____

Life Re-Imagined Journal

Life Re-Imagined Journal

_____

_____

_____

_____

_____

_____

_____

_____

_____

_____

_____

_____

_____

_____

_____

_____

_____

_____

_____

_____

_____

_____

_____

Life Re-Imagined Journal

_____

_____

_____

_____

_____

_____

_____

_____

_____

_____

_____

_____

_____

_____

_____

_____

_____

_____

_____

_____

_____

_____

_____

_____

Life Re-Imagined Journal

Life Re-Imagined Journal

_____

_____

_____

_____

_____

_____

_____

_____

_____

_____

_____

_____

_____

_____

_____

_____

_____

_____

_____

_____

_____

_____

Life Re-Imagined Journal

_____

_____

_____

_____

_____

_____

_____

_____

_____

_____

_____

_____

_____

_____

_____

_____

_____

_____

_____

_____

_____

_____

_____

Life Re-Imagined Journal

_____

_____

_____

_____

_____

_____

_____

_____

_____

_____

_____

_____

_____

_____

_____

_____

_____

_____

_____

_____

_____

_____

_____

_____

Life Re-Imagined Journal

_____

_____

_____

_____

_____

_____

_____

_____

_____

_____

_____

_____

_____

_____

_____

_____

_____

_____

_____

_____

_____

_____

_____

Life Re-Imagined Journal

_____

_____

_____

_____

_____

_____

_____

_____

_____

_____

_____

_____

_____

_____

_____

_____

_____

_____

_____

_____

_____

_____

_____

Life Re-Imagined Journal

_____

_____

_____

_____

_____

_____

_____

_____

_____

_____

_____

_____

_____

_____

_____

_____

_____

_____

_____

_____

_____

_____

_____

_____

_____

_____

_____

Life Re-Imagined Journal

_____

_____

_____

_____

_____

_____

_____

_____

_____

_____

_____

_____

_____

_____

_____

_____

_____

_____

_____

_____

_____

_____

_____

Life Re-Imagined Journal

\

\

\

\

\

\

\

\

\

\

\

\

\

\

\

\

\

\

\

\

\

\

\

\

Life Re-Imagined Journal

_____

_____

_____

_____

_____

_____

_____

_____

_____

_____

_____

_____

_____

_____

_____

_____

_____

_____

_____

_____

Life Re-Imagined Journal

_____

_____

_____

_____

_____

_____

_____

_____

_____

_____

_____

_____

_____

_____

_____

_____

_____

_____

_____

_____

_____

_____

_____

Life Re-Imagined Journal

_____

_____

_____

_____

_____

_____

_____

_____

_____

_____

_____

_____

_____

_____

_____

_____

_____

_____

_____

_____

_____

_____

_____

_____

Life Re-Imagined Journal

_____

_____

_____

_____

_____

_____

_____

_____

_____

_____

_____

_____

_____

_____

_____

_____

_____

_____

_____

_____

_____

_____

_____

_____

_____

Life Re-Imagined Journal

Life Re-Imagined Journal

Life Re-Imagined Journal

_____

_____

_____

_____

_____

_____

_____

_____

_____

_____

_____

_____

_____

_____

_____

_____

_____

_____

_____

_____

_____

_____

_____

_____

_____

_____

_____

Life Re-Imagined Journal

_____

_____

_____

_____

_____

_____

_____

_____

_____

_____

_____

_____

_____

_____

_____

_____

_____

_____

_____

_____

_____

_____

_____

_____

_____

_____

Life Re-Imagined Journal

_____
_____
_____
_____
_____
_____
_____
_____
_____
_____
_____
_____
_____
_____
_____
_____
_____
_____
_____
_____
_____
_____
_____

Life Re-Imagined Journal

Life Re-Imagined Journal

Life Re-Imagined Journal

Life Re-Imagined Journal

_____

_____

_____

_____

_____

_____

_____

_____

_____

_____

_____

_____

_____

_____

_____

_____

_____

_____

_____

_____

_____

_____

_____

Life Re-Imagined Journal

_____

_____

_____

_____

_____

_____

_____

_____

_____

_____

_____

_____

_____

_____

_____

_____

_____

_____

_____

_____

_____

_____

_____

_____

_____

_____

_____

Life Re-Imagined Journal

Life Re-Imagined Journal

_____

_____

_____

_____

_____

_____

_____

_____

_____

_____

_____

_____

_____

_____

_____

_____

_____

_____

_____

_____

_____

_____

Life Re-Imagined Journal

_____

_____

_____

_____

_____

_____

_____

_____

_____

_____

_____

_____

_____

_____

_____

_____

_____

_____

_____

_____

_____

_____

_____

_____

Life Re-Imagined Journal

Keitra Robinson is an award winning speaker, life & leadership strategist, certified Human Behavior Consultant, and founder of Justinspire Legends™ LLC, a personal and professional development company based in Orlando, Florida. Before aligning her career to the business of inspiring and equipping leaders and women to "Be Great...On Purpose"™, Keitra's career as a lawyer, mediator and leader offered a valuable segue into her current role. Having spent the majority of her legal career providing leadership to attorneys and mediating professionals, she successfully led and coached her teams to achieving consistent high performance recognitions for programs under her leadership. Perhaps most importantly, she discovered all the more her passion and heart for leadership expressed through foundations she terms as "inspirational competence"™", one area of which as a leadership strategist, she now coaches and trains.

As a leadership and executive coach, Keitra's coaching practice focuses on empowering women to lead in their various spheres of influence with vision, strategy, skill, confidence, and an effectiveness that draws from and develops the unique gifts and talents each woman brings to the table. As a life strategist, she commits to help women re-imagine their lives to greater paths of purpose and fulfillment. Keitra has established her voice in encouraging a culture of visionary women.

A trained formally coach and certified human behavior consultant, she has garnered foundations through significant training and experiences aligned with the gold standard of coaching excellence established through the International Coaching Federation and is a graduate of the Christian Coach Institute. Keitra is also a magna cum laude graduate of North Carolina Central University and a graduate of Pepperdine University School of Law where she obtained both her Juris Doctorate degree and certification in conflict resolution from the #1 nationally ranked Straus Institute for Alternative Dispute Resolution.

Booking Information

Justinspire Legends LLC
To learn more about Keitra and to view a sample of her speaker presentations:
www.KeitraRobinson.com

To inquire about corporate, conference, or church speaker bookings:
www.KeitraRobinson.com/request-Keitra

or

email: info@justinspirelegends.com

Executive and Leadership Coaching Inquiries:
Keitra@justinspirelegends.com

To Stay Connected

Facebook & Instagram:
KeitraRobinsonSpeaks

LinkedIn:
Keitra Robinson, JD, CHBC

Women's Faith & Empowerment Facebook Community:
Facebook @Shine360Women

Made in the USA
Columbia, SC
17 August 2019